A PSYCHOLOGICAL INTERPRETATION OF RUTH
BY
YEHEZKEL KLUGER

STANDING IN THE SANDALS OF
NAOMI
BY NOMI KLUGER-NASH

A Psychological Interpretation of

RUTH

In the Light of Mythology,
Legend and Kabbalah

by Yehezkel Kluger

———————————

Companion Essay:

Standing in the Sandals of

NAOMI

by Nomi Kluger-Nash

DAIMON

Cover picture: drawing by Shraga Weil,
from *Song of Solomon*, Workers Book Guild, Israel

ISBN 3-85630-587-4

Copyright © 1999 by Daimon Verlag,
Am Klosterplatz, CH-8840 Einsiedeln, Switzerland

Printed in Canada

Contents

Standing in the Sandals of Naomi
by Nomi Kluger-Nash

Introduction

1. Psychology and the Bible

The present subject matter is an investigation and interpretation of a biblical book in the light of Jungian psychology. I hope to show its findings to be pertinent to the theme of the fate and role of the feminine.

It is no disparagement of the Holy Writ to read it with psychological understanding. Many biblical texts reveal unsuspected dimensions when approached with modern psychological insight. Jung wrote: "We must read the Bible or we shall not understand psychology."[1] One such text is the Book of Ruth, which has engaged the interest of laymen and scholars throughout the ages right up to the present. Reading the Book of Ruth in this light, and in its original context, reveals a process remarkably appropriate to the modern view of the place of woman, and of the feminine principle itself.

The original version of this work, printed as "A Contribution to the Study of the Feminine Principle in the Old Testament,"[2] was stimulated by a series of lectures by Rivkah Schärf on "Women in the Old Testament"[3].

---

[1] The Visions Seminars, vol. 1, p. 156.
[2] Subsequently published in condensed form in *Spring,* 1957.
[3] Rivkah Kluger, *Jl. Analyt. Psychol.,* Vol. 23, No. 2, 1978, pp. 135-148.

2. History and Myth

In the numerous commentaries, the only point on which all agree is the beauty of the story and of its literary style. Goethe's remark[4] referring to it as "the loveliest little epic and idyllic whole which has come down to us," is frequently quoted. True as this may be, it is certain that the book was not included in the Canon merely because of its literary merit. Some scholars, find more or less apparent mythological motifs in the story, and deny it any historical validity. Others, point out the essential harmony of the story with the historical time it portrays, and see no reason for the Hebrews to invent a despised heathen ancestry for David, founder of the royal line, and deny it mythological significance.

Historical and archeological investigations indicate the universality of mythical motifs from prehistoric times onwards. Mythological motifs are, as Jung has demonstrated, symbolical expressions of basic forces of psychic life.[5] He called these forces archetypes. "The essential content of all mythologies and all religions and all isms is archetypal." (CW8, ¶406) Archetypes are the innate basic contents of the unconscious, the "universal, formative patterns of potential behavior and meaning-making (which) pulse beneath the surface of consciousness." [6]

Today it is no longer necessary to insist on the profound rôle of the unconscious. Insofar as there is any developmental tendency or urge in the life of man, we find it expressed in (if not indeed induced by) his unconscious processes. We observe this in the individual in his dreams – and in a people, in their myths and legends. These portray not only universal patterns

---

[4] Westöstlicher Divan: Hebräer.

[5] "Myth is the primordial language natural to ... psychic processes, and no intellectual formulation comes anywhere near the richness and expressiveness of mythical imagery" (CW12, ¶ 28).

[6] S. A. Martin, in *Quadrant, The Journal of Contemporary Jungian Thought,* XXIV: 2, 1991, p. 5.

of human behavior, but a direction, even a goal, toward which man seems to be impelled, pushed or led. The study of myths, fairy tales, and dreams, all of which contain archetypal images, indicate a direction toward the development of a fuller consciousness, (not without dangers, reversals and setbacks) The goal is an integration of psychic contents directed toward a presumable attainment of ultimate wholeness. The study of history also shows a similar striving toward a desired goal. The least we can say is that psychic and objective events stand in some relationship to each other.

History and mythology are not always so clearly separable. A biblical figure or event may be a historical fact, or a mythological motif – which is a psychic fact no less real than a historical one – or it may be an actual person or occurrence around which, in the course of time, mythological or legendary qualities grow. This can happen when the event particularly fits or expresses an archetypal theme. We might even say that the archetype "expressed itself" in the individual or event. Archetypes not only influence man's actions, but may take over the whole man or situation. "Perhaps," in Jung's words, "we may sum up this general phenomenon as *Ergriffenheit* – a state of being seized or possessed. The term postulates not only an *Ergriffener* (one who is seized) but an *Ergreiffer* (one who seizes)." (CW10, ¶386) In such a case it is the archetype itself which is lived, in which case history and mythology are virtually identical.

That a people was freed from bondage by a God Who, appearing to them in flame and smoke, gave them a new law and led them through a dangerous wilderness to a land flowing with milk and honey, is a myth. But that the Hebrews who had been slaves in Egypt came thence through a desert into a fertile land, bringing with them, under Moses' guidance, a new spiritual religion, is history.

That David was a king in Israel, founder of the royal line; that he extended the borders of the country, pushing back the powerful Philistines; that over thousands of years, for millions of people he was and is considered the forerunner of the Messiah, is historical fact. That David, a boy hero, slew the Philistine giant Goliath; that a divine redeemer would spring from his seed, is myth.

In a biblical story historical and mythological elements may be interwoven, yet neither need invalidate the other. Both may contribute to the same psychological truth. Archetypes can manifest themselves historically, or differently put, we might even say that history is, by and large, the manifestation of archetypes.

Through changes in history, changes in beliefs, attitudes, values, we may glimpse the change in the development of archetypal images. These images come into being due to the interaction between the conscious and the unconscious – a development which alone can make history, and our own share in it, meaningful.

It is through an examination of its archetypal configuration that we shall attempt to understand the story of Ruth. To this end we will view it as a myth, i.e., a psychic representation. We shall take cognizance of its psychic and historical context (the Bible and the Hebrews), and its relation to myths of the surrounding peoples. To help us penetrate to its psychological meaning, we will also take into account the legends which later attached to it, since these may be considered to constitute a "commentary by the psyche of a people." The psyche is understood as including both conscious and unconscious processes.

I believe that this examination of the Book of Ruth from a psychological, mythical perspective, reveals an unsuspected dimension of this beautiful and popular book.

3. Synopsis of the Book of Ruth

Chapter 1. Because of a famine in the land of Judah, Elimelech, his wife Naomi, and their two sons, Mahlon and

Chilion, leave Bethlehem and go to Moab. There Elimelech dies. HIs sons marry Moabite women, Ruth and Orpah. After about ten years the sons also die. Having heard of the cessation of the famine, Naomi sets out for Bethlehem, her daughters-in-law accompanying her. She urges them to turn back to their people where they might yet find husbands, for she could offer them no such hope. After tearful protestations, Orpah turns back, but Ruth cleaves to Naomi. The two women arrive at Bethlehem at the beginning of the barley harvest. Naomi complains to the women of the city, who are surprised to see her, of the bitterness of her loss.

Chapter 2. Ruth sets out to glean and arrives by chance on the field of Boaz, a kinsman of Elimelech. On coming to his field, Boaz inquires about her. He treats her with great kindness, urges her to remain on his field only, invites her to eat at mealtime, and instructs his workers to leave rich gleaning for her. Returning home well supplied, she tells her mother-in-law of her experiences. Naomi informs her that Boaz is one of their redeeming kinsmen, and that she should continue gleaning on his field, which Ruth does to the end of the harvest, dwelling with her mother-in-law.

Chapter 3. Naomi, concerned for Ruth's welfare, instructs her to wash, anoint and dress herself, and go to the threshing floor where Boaz is winnowing that night; to remain hidden, and marking where he lies down after eating and drinking, to uncover his feet, lie down, and follow his instructions. Boaz awakens at midnight to find Ruth there. She asks him to marry her in accordance with his obligation as a redeeming kinsman. He blesses her that she did "not turn to younger men," and promises her to fulfill her request provided a nearer kinsman, with a prior right, does not exercise it. He sends her away before dawn with a gift of barley for Naomi, who advises Ruth to sit still "… for the man will not rest, but will settle the matter today."

Chapter 4. At the city gate, in the presence of ten elders, Boaz asks the nearer kinsman if he is ready to redeem the land of Elimelech by buying it from Naomi. He says yes. Boaz then raises the related duty of marrying Ruth "to perpetuate the name of the deceased upon his estate," whereupon the nearer kinsman relinquishes his rights to Boaz, who calls the people to witness his purchase of the land and marriage to Ruth. The people bless Boaz and Ruth, invoking the names of Rachel and Leah, the matriarchs of Israel, and of Tamar and Judah, the parents of Perez. A son is born of their union, at which the women congratulate Naomi, who becomes nurse to him. They name him Obed. He is the father of Jesse, the father of David. A genealogy from Perez to David closes the book.

4. The Basic Pattern of the Seasonal Myth

It is not self-evident from a cursory reading of the Book of Ruth that the story may be seen as a myth, but let us look at it a bit more closely. Throughout the ancient world, from Babylonia to Rome, there are to be found a number of myths in which the theme of the annual decay and revival of vegetation is readily discernible; which is not to say that they are merely allegories of the seasonal occurrences. "... the psyche ... mirrors our empirical world only in part ... The archetype ... describes how the psyche experiences the physical fact." (CW 9i, ¶260) Such, for example are the so-called seasonal myths about Tammuz and Ishtar, Attis and Kybele, Adonis and Astarte, Osiris and Isis, and Demeter and Persephone. They, and the seasonal rituals which accompany them, adhere to a basic pattern, as Theodore Gaster has demonstrated.[7] They "fall into two clear divisions of *Kenosis,* or Emptying, and *Plerosis,* or Filling, the former representing the

---

[7] T. H. Gaster, *Thespis: Ritual, Myth, and Drama in the Ancient Near East.* 2 Doubleday & Company, Garden City, N. Y., 1961. (Cited from 1st ed., 1950)

evacuation of life, the latter its replenishment." This is clearly the case also in the Book of Ruth, which opens with famine and death, and closes with harvest and birth.

The Book of Ruth is radically different from the typical Tammuz-Adonis-Osiris type of myth, but we can easily find traces of the typical pattern.[8] This is not to say that "Ruth" was derived from these myths, but it does hint at a common archetypal ancestry. The comparable features permit us, via the outspoken myths, to delineate the common archetypal (i.e., mythical) pattern of our story.

It is at once apparent that "Ruth" is no mere variation of seasonal myths, no more than the Hebrew religion was merely a variation of the surrounding pagan religions. But just as the biblical story of the flood, which contains motifs also present in an earlier Sumerian myth, is transformed in a manner reflecting the Hebrew religious genius and representing a further spiritual development, just so the Ruth story has its clear affinity with pagan mythology. In the course of this presentation some of these connections will be brought out more clearly. The foregoing was to indicate that, transformed in content though it be, "Ruth" adheres in general lines to a basic mythological pattern. Like all myths, it is an archetypal expression, more or less complete, of a process in the collective unconscious. To see what this process is, let us look at the story more closely.

---

[8] The outstanding features of the pattern are, per Gaster, under *Kenosis*:
Mortification: deposition or slaying of the king.
Ululation: lamentation and weeping.
Purgation: expulsion of evil influences or scapegoats.
and under *Plerosis*,
Invigoration: a ritual combat, and/or the sacred marriage (hieros gamos)
Jubilation: joyous celebration of new-won life, re-instatement of the king, or birth of the savior-god.

Chapter One

1. The Initial Situation of the Story

> In the days when the judges ruled, there was a famine in the land; and a man of Bethlehem in Judah, with his wife and two sons, went to reside in the country of Moab. (1:1)

The time of the story is set in the days of the judges, that is, after the age of the patriarchs and after the leadership of Moses, when the psyche of the people had already been molded by the crucible of the wandering in the wilderness and by the new law they had received there, their covenant with Yahweh. But now something is wrong. The times are out of joint. The land is unfruitful. Instead of life there is the threat of death, and a family must flee into exile.

A famine, as an "act of God," represents a disorder in the relationship between man and God. Man's well-being depends on his obedience to God's law. This is specifically stated in Leviticus:

> If you will follow My laws and faithfully observe My commandments, I will grant your rains in their season, so that the earth shall yield its produce.... you shall eat your fill of bread, and dwell securely in your land.... But if you do not obey Me and do not observe all these commandments ... I will set My face against you.... Your land shall not yield its produce.
>
> Lev. 26:3-20

Put into psychological language, a famine, in this context, represents a disturbance in the relationship between ego-consciousness and the Self (the archetype of wholeness, at once the center and totality of the entire psyche, conscious plus unconscious, superordinate and transcendent to the ego). (CW 6, ¶790). If a man is cut off from the unconscious (his psychic basis), his conscious ground becomes sterile, unfruitful. To regain nourishment he must seek it across the border, in the other land, in the unconscious. There he may find that which is necessary for his well being.

In our story it is a family which crosses the border into a foreign land, a family of four. As Jung has abundantly demonstrated[9], the number four is a symbol of wholeness, of totality, and within this symbol there is a matter of arrangement. The ideally balanced whole consists of pairs of opposites. In the present quaternity we find a certain imbalance, three men as against one woman. To find the reason for this we have to go back to before the "days when the judges ruled."

In the Hebrew religion the Great Mother Goddess was dethroned. Yahweh is a God having no wife and born of no woman. This well nigh miraculous step in the development of the concept of God, was constantly threatened, as the Bible frequently attests, by backsliding to pagan practices. To safeguard the new concept the feminine principle was severely repressed, with a consequent emphasis on the masculine.

In her essay "Old Testament Roots of Woman's Spiritual Problem," Rivkah Kluger writes:

"In the pre-biblical polytheistic era the feminine principle was dominant. It was the time of the great mother-goddesses, whose life-rhythm was a cyclic eternal return of fertility and destruction, as the law of nature ... In (the) ambivalent praise of ... the greatly loved and greatly feared goddess (h)er destructive power comes more and more to the fore, especially

---

[9] CW 9i, ¶426; CW 11, ¶¶ 136, 176; CW12, ¶327; CW16, ¶404f.; and many more.

in several hero myths where the motif of overcoming the great mother becomes *the* central heroic task ... (for she is) threatening to annihilate the masculine principle. The hero must free his masculinity from the embrace of the devouring mother.

"The time of the sun-god, of a new consciousness ... freeing itself from the eternal cyclic return of the same, leads to a dynamic image of a god who contains all aspects of divine nature, united in a single god-personality – a unity full of tension between the opposites, which leads to conflict and consciousness...."

In the beginning of the Hebrew religion with its marked contrast to the polytheism containing a strong wife and/or mother goddess, it was just this unique masculine differentiating spirit (in contrast to the feminine embracing, containing, one), which had such difficulty in becoming established. This is shown by the long barrenness of Sarah ("can Sarah bear a child at ninety?" Gen. 17:17), and Rebekah (Isaac pleaded with the Lord on behalf of his wife, for she was barren. Gen. 25:21). Rivkah Kluger writes: "The Old Testament God, a dynamic God who forces man into a process of growing consciousness, is a religious novum.... This happening in the divine archetypal world had deep and far-reaching psychological consequences for women. The pagan nature-boundness, which is innate in women, had to yield to a history-creating development.... (Women) were deprived of their inner basis, of being contained in the mother-cult." (pp. 135f.)

It was precisely because of the difficulty with which it came into being, and because of the continual danger of the spiritual masculinity being swallowed up again (cf. the constant backsliding in the desert,[10] even to the longing for the slavery in Egypt, i.e., being possessed by the unconscious), that the more natural, nature-bound, feminine had to be so strongly

---

[10] Ex. 14:11f., 16:3, 17:3, 32:8, Numb. 11:4f., 11:18ff., 14:1ff., 20:5, 21:5, 25:1, 31:15f.

repressed. In our story the emphasis on the masculine element in the conscious side of the Hebrew psyche is reflected in the composition of Elimelech's family.

This one-sided structure gives us a clue about the reason for the famine, for it is the feminine which is the nurturing side. Interestingly enough, Bethlehem is normally one of the most fruitful districts of Judah, and the name of the city could mean "house of bread." However it may be the "house of the god Lahmu," Lehem being the equivalent of this Babylonian god.[11] But now there is no bread, the land does not yield its fruit, the situation is unhealthy. The unhealthy situation is confirmed by the names of the sons. In mythology the names of the characters are usually meaningful and significant for the story, which is also the case here.

> The man's name was Elimelech, his wife's name was Naomi, and his two sons were named Mahlon and Chilion – Ephratites of Bethlehem in Judah. They came to the country of Moab and remained there. (1:2)

Elimelech means "My God is king," and since this is the Hebrew people, it is Yahweh to whom they are subject, the entirely masculine God, free of feminine connections; no mother, no wife.

Naomi, from the root *na'am*, "pleasant," means "my delight," "my sweetness," as well as "my pleasant one." "Charm," "bliss," are also contained in it. Although it appears also in masculine forms, the name, full of feeling, is an expression of the feminine eros quality. Some scholars[12] see a direct relation between Naomi and Naaman, which was the Phoenician name for Adonis, and means "my beloved." The flowers that sprang from his blood are anemones, from the same root. But despite other links between the story of Ruth

---

[11] cf. W. E. Staples, "The Book of Ruth," A. J. S. L. 53, 1937, p. 149.

[12] Besides the views of various commentators (see bibliography), the lexicons used are Koehler-Baumgartner and Gesenius.

and the Adonis myth, this association by a common root, via Naomi's name, is not convincing, and is disputed on philological grounds.

Mahlon, from the root *holeh*, "sick," means simply sickness. It is possible that the name is derived from a different root, the Arabic *mhl*, according to W. Rudolph, which would then give it the meaning "unfruitfulness"[13]. The first is the accepted derivation, although the latter fits our story just as well.

Chilion comes from a root with several stems: "vanishing," "consumption," "languishing," are the meanings it has. Some of the derivatives of the root are: cease, vanish, perish, consume, terminate, destroy.

Two features thus stand out in this family, this quaternity: an overweight on the masculine side, and a loss of vitality in the new generation. This condition parallels the state of their ground: "there was a famine in the land." But what was the nature of the land they went to?

2. The Nature of Moab

The Moabites were a once related but subsequently estranged part of the family of the Hebrews, a part that had gone a different way. They were the descendants of Lot, Abraham's nephew. So the myth tells us, and so too, does history. Archeological evidence indicates that "the Moabites and the Ammonites were at one time not differentiated from the Hebrews, or rather that all three belonged to a single group. Hebrew and Moabitish and Ammonitish (languages) stood in ... close relationship to one another.... the political relations continued to be hostile from the first differentiation of the three groups."[14]

---

[13] The Arabic *mhl*, W. Rudolph, Das Buch Ruth, in K. A. T., Leipzig, 1939, p. 16.
[14] M. Jastrow Jr., Dictionary of the Bible, extra vol, pp. 73ff.

Abraham and Lot went together from Ur of the Chaldeans, westward to Canaan (Gen. 11:31, 12:5). They dwelt together until their herdsmen quarreled. Then came a parting of their ways, and the subsequent development of the peoples that stemmed from them. Abraham offered Lot the choice of which way he would go.

> So Lot chose for himself the whole plain of the Jordan, and Lot journeyed eastward. Thus they parted from each other....
> Lot ... pitching his tents near Sodom.
>   Gen. 13:11f.

Lot went *east*, back in the direction he had come from, i.e., a regression toward the polytheistic mother-goddess culture, to a city which was doomed. Earlier Lot had accompanied Abraham who had gone to Canaan at the instigation of Yahweh. (Gen. 12:4). He had originally followed the new masculine development with his paternal uncle, and so Yahweh rescued him from the destruction of Sodom. But even when God's messengers warned him to escape,

> he delayed. So the men seized his hand, and the hands of his wife and his two daughters – in the Lord's mercy on him – and brought him out and left him outside the city.... one said, "Flee for your life! Do not look behind you...."
>   Gen. 19:16f.

Here again, as in our story, we meet a family of four, a quaternity, but this time the emphasis is on the feminine side. Lot's reluctance to leave the old behind was outdone by his wife, who, gazing back despite the warning, was turned into a pillar of salt, and so was cut off from any new life.

Yet a second, and even a third step back into the realm of the feminine, are the preludes to the beginning of Moab.

> Lot ... and his two daughters lived in a cave. And the older one said to the younger: "Come, let us make our father drink wine, and let us lie with him, that we may maintain life through our father." That night they made their father drink wine, and the

older daughter went in and lay with her father; he did not know when she lay down or when she rose.

Gen. 19:30-33

Out of this father-daughter incest was born Moab, the father of the Moabites. (The younger daughter bore Ben-Ami, the father of the Ammonites.) The cave needs no elaboration as a feminine symbol. Lot went into the very womb of the mother to live, into the unconscious. And beyond that, at the very conception of Moab, Lot was still deeper in that realm of the feminine; he was unconscious.

It must be noted that the purpose of this incest was to "preserve the seed of our father" (as the older translations put it), that is, the masculine – symbolically, the conscious, the differentiating spirit. And it was through the use of wine, a spiritous liquor, that it was achieved. Legend even has it that God put the wine in the cave so that the daughters should succeed in their plan.[15] This was done, however, under the aegis of the "mother" – in the cave – and at the instigation of the daughters. The masculine was preserved, but under feminine domination. This motif of the masculine spirit overpowered by the feminine is more clearly to be seen in a parallel mythologem, the story of the birth of Adonis.[16]

Like Lot's daughters, Myrrha, the daughter of king Kinyras of Cyprus, made her father drunk and slept with him. The child born of this incest was Adonis. Though a male god, he was in thrall to two goddesses, Aphrodite and Persephone. Like his Babylonian counterpart, Tammuz, this dying and resurrecting god is a god of women especially. Women mourn his annual death, and rejoice at his rebirth. (A biblical reference to this pagan custom is found in Ezekiel 8:14. The prophet was brought in a vision to the temple in Jerusalem, "and there sat the women bewailing Tammuz.") They also

---

[15] Louis Ginzberg, *The Legends of the Jews*, The Jewish Publication Society, Philadelphia, 1947. Vol. v, p. 243

[16] C. Kerényi, *The Gods of the Greeks*, Thames and Hudson, London, 1951. pp75f.

offer him their chastity. His time is divided between *the* goddess in two of her aspects: the benevolent, nourishing love goddess (Aphrodite, Ishtar), and the underworld goddess, queen of the realm of the dead (Persephone, Ereshkigal). The worship of Adonis, like that of Tammuz, is associated with the worship of the love goddess.

Moab was not a god like Adonis, but he was the legendary ancestor of a whole people. In both Bible and legend we find this people associated, if not outright with a love goddess, nevertheless with passion, or more accurately put, with licentiousness. Chemosh was the god of the Moabites mentioned in the Bible (1 Kings 11:7). But there is also a record of an Astarte-Chemosh[17]. About the love goddess in Greek mythology, Kerényi (p. 67) writes: "She is the same deity as our oriental neighbors worshipped under such barbarian names as Ishtar or Ashtaroth, which we later reproduced as Astarte. In the East she was a goddess who made peculiarly strong amorous demands, but was also abundantly generous with the pleasures of love." Astarte, later termed Aphrodite, is the goddess in the Adonis myth. Legend says that Chemosh was a black stone in the form of a woman (Ginzberg, iii, p. 352). In the Bible we first meet the Moabites as a nation toward the end of the wandering of the Hebrews through the desert.

> While Israel was staying at Shittim, the people profaned themselves by whoring with the Moabite women.
>
> Numb. 25:1

The Moabites had joined with the Midianites on this occasion in fear of the approaching Israelites, calling on Balaam to curse them (Numb. 22:3-6). This Balaam was unable to do, but he did advise them to seduce the Israelites, according to legend which is based on this and other biblical passages. Thus Yahweh tells the Israelites to smite the Midianites

---

[17] D. B., vol. iii, p. 403.

... for they assailed you by the trickery they practiced against you
– because of the affair of Peor and because of the affair of their
kinswoman Cozbi, daughter of the Midianite chieftain ...

Numb. 25:16

Later, when the Israelites were victorious in war with the
Midianites, Moses was wroth with the commanders of the
returning army, saying:

"You have spared every female! Yet they are the very ones who, at
the bidding of Balaam, induced the Israelites to trespass against
the Lord in the matter of Peor ..."

Numb. 31:15f

The legend tells how old Moabite women, sitting at the
entrance to their tents at Shittim, offered fine linen garments
to passing Israelites, and encouraged them to enter to see still
more beautiful wares. Inside lovely young, perfumed, girls
offered linens at little cost, and pointed out their common
descent from Terah (father of Abraham, grandfather of Lot).
They served them wine, kindled their passion, and then
seduced the men, involving them in the worship of their god
Peor by having them bow before the idol in the act of
undressing. Ginzberg (vi, p. 134f.) draws attention to the
Revelation of St. John, 2:14, which likely presupposes a
knowledge of this legend.

... thou hast them there that hold the doctrine of Balaam, who
taught Balac (king of Moab) to cast a stumbling block before the
children of Israel, to eat things and sacrifice unto idols and
commit fornication.

In the legend, insofar as sexual intercourse is linked with
idolatry, it is reminiscent of the hierodules or sacred prostitutes who functioned in the service of Tammuz and Ishtar,
Adonis and Aphrodite, etc. It is told that God had earlier
offered the Torah, the Teachings, to the Moabites, but when
they learned that it commanded "thou shalt not commit
unchastity," they refused to accept it (Ginzberg, iii, p. 81).

The very water at Shittim caused unchastity for it came from the "Well of Lewdness," a well which would dry up only in the Messianic time (ibid. p. 382).

These legends give us an idea of the negative view toward the feminine then extant. Since polytheism, containing the goddess as a central figure, was the direct antithesis to monotheism, eros, as the essence of feeling, of feminine relatedness, which the goddess also symbolized, was seen in its negatively eroticized aspect. The worship of the goddess was an act of unfaithfulness towards Yahweh, so was characterized as harlotry, unchastity. And because the goddess was excluded, the feminine principle, as embodied in Woman, was, to a certain extent alienated for the Hebrews.

In our story Moab represents the psychic opposite or complement to Israel. A hunger, a famine, causes a family symbolizing a totality, with an overweight on the masculine (logos) side, to move to a land which is characterized by a corresponding but opposite overweight on the feminine (eros) side.

3. The Threat of the Feminine for the Masculine

The psychic climate of this land was not, apparently, favorable for the continued existence of the masculine element.

> Elimelech, Naomi's husband, died; and she was left with her two sons. They married Moabite women, one named Orpah and the other Ruth, and they lived there about ten years. Then those two – Mahlon and Chilion – also died; so the woman was left without her two sons and without her husband. (1:3-5)

The men die. However, of the original quaternity, all has not quite disappeared. Naomi still remains. And, as we shall see later, a spiritual heir to the dead can again be raised.

We have a certain parallelism in this with the Adonis-Tammuz myths. The death and rebirth of these gods marks the seasonal death and rebirth of vegetation. In our story these incidents are related to famine and harvest. During his death the god is in the underworld, when alive, back on earth. Moab and Judah would be corresponding places in our story. Winckler (p. 66) sees Ruth uniting both aspects of the goddess – the death bringing virginal Kore, queen of the underworld, – and wife of the re-awakening god, lord of fruitful nature. Naomi too, has certain Ishtar similarities: her husband dies, she mourns, only later to rejoice amid public jubilation at the birth of a restorer of life. Boaz, as we shall see later in more detail, has certain Tammuz features.

But the parallel between our story and the Adonis-Tammuz myths cannot be drawn too closely, and those who attempt it get into difficulties in placing the characters. Tammuz, or Adonis, is now Elimelech, now Mahlon or Chilion, then Boaz, and again Obed. And similarly with the goddess figure. It all becomes rather muddled when too close a parallel is sought. The fact cited by Jeremias that Bethlehem was the site of a grove dedicated to Adonis, as reported by St. Jerome [340?-420 C. E.] (p. 223), after his visit there, is not in itself sufficient evidence that our story is basically an Adonis myth.

Ruth is decidedly not merely a disguised Tammuz-Adonis type myth, but viewing it against that background permits an appreciation of the profound cultural change or development portrayed by our story, from the stage of matriarchal domination these myths portray. The extent of this domination can be gauged by the image of Ishtar in the Gilgamesh Epic. The great goddess is enraged when Gilgamesh reminds her that, among other evils, "For Tammuz, thy youthful husband, thou hast decreed wailing year after year." (Heidel, p. 51) She complains (but without any hint of remorse) to her father, the heavenly Anu, that "Gilgamesh has enumerated my stinking deeds and my rotten acts" (p. 52), and insists on his creating "the bull of heaven that he may destroy Gilgamesh," threaten-

ing to release the dead from the underworld if he refuses. He
accedes to her demand.

Naomi, meaning "pleasant," is not simply the positive
aspect of an all-powerful Ishtar. She is the feminine component of the Hebrew psyche insofar as it is pictured in our
original quaternity – outnumbered, i.e., reduced in importance, vis-a-vis the masculine element.

Equally if not more important is the fact that she is devoted
to the patriarchal culture of which she is a part, and to its
spiritual, not merely male, God. This is what sets her off from
the more nature-bound femininity of the Ishtar or Astarte-
Aphrodite type. These were the goddesses who emasculated
their followers, whether literally, like Attis (Kerényi, p. 90), or
figuratively. The priests of the goddess were often eunuchs or
were made impotent (Apuleius, p. 199). In contrast, the
Hebrews forbade any man who was blemished, sexually or
otherwise, to engage in priestly duties (Lev. 21:16ff.). The
goddess was dangerous to the man. We have only to recall
what Gilgamesh said to Ishtar when she wooed him. "What
will be my advantage if I take thee in marriage?" he asked, and
answered himself: "Thou art but a palace which crushes the
heroes within it." (Heidel, p. 50) Moab represented such a
danger. If the overweighted masculinity of the Hebrews found
their own earth becoming barren, they found the overweighted femininity of Moab to be absolutely fatal.

One might have expected that with their marriage, Mahlon
and Chilion would prosper and beget children. Instead they
were cut off childless. This union with the feminine of Moab
in Moab, did not restore them, for in those times, to leave
their own land was to leave their own God (Smith, p. 36).

The danger to the new masculine principle in leaving its
own land is illustrated in the patriarchal sagas. Abraham seems
to have been well aware of this danger when he charged his
servant to go back to his old land to fetch a wife for his son
Isaac.

And the servant said to him, "What if the woman does not consent to follow me to this land, shall I then take your son back to the land from which you came?" Abraham answered him, *"On no account must you take my son back there!* The Lord, the God of heaven, who took me from my father's house and from my native land, who promised me on oath, saying, 'I will assign this land to your offspring' – He will send His angel before you, and you will get a wife for my son from there. And if the woman does not consent to follow you, you shall then be clear of this oath to me; *but do not take my son back there."*

Gen. 24:5-8

This danger is borne out in our story by the deaths of the two men. But the feminine principle, curtailed though it was in the Hebrew psyche, was not eliminated. Naomi still remains, and as already remarked, she was loyal to Yahweh.

4. The Challenge of the Masculine for the Feminine

A shift toward the feminine took place in our family with the marriage of the sons. Through the addition of the foreign women, the masculine was even overcompensated. By the deaths of Mahlon and Chilion this enantiodromia or shift toward the counterpole, reached the totally opposite, and immediately a countermovement toward the masculine begins.

She started out with her daughters-in-law to return from the country of Moab; for in the country of Moab she had heard that the Lord had taken note of His people and given them food.

(1:6)

It is striking that she learns of the end of the famine just after her sons die. Could it be that there is an inner connection? It is as though the death of the "sickly" and "consumptive" offspring were a prerequisite for God "taking note of his people and giving them food." As frequently occurs in psychic processes, new life follows only after the death of the old. This is, in fact, a psychic law, attested to by countless myths, dreams, and other psychic products. We see it in all the so-called seasonal myths already referred to. The alchemists, whose work was really a projection of psychic processes into matter, say that no new life can arise without the death of the old. In the alchemical work *Rosarium Philosophorum* the illustration (reproduced in CW 16, p. 259) picturing death is called "Conception." In our story too, the deaths of the sons mark a new beginning.

> Accompanied by her two daughters-in-law, she left the place where she had been living; and they set out on the road back to the land of Judah. (1:7)

Naomi starts back from "the place where she had been living," namely the land of the pagan feminine, to return to "the land of Judah," the land of Yahweh and His people. But she is not alone. Through her sons' marriages a new, a foreign femininity, has become attached to her, and accompanies her. Nevertheless, Naomi sends them back.

> But Naomi said to her two daughters-in-law, "Turn back, each of you to her mother's house. May the Lord deal kindly with you, as you have dealt with the dead and with me! May the Lord grant that each of you find security in the house of a husband!" And she kissed them farewell. They broke into weeping. (1:8, 9)

Note that she tells them to return to their mothers' house. The usual biblical expression for the domicile of an unmarried woman is the father's house, as we would expect in a patriarchal society. That Ruth and Orpah are referred back to their mothers' houses is another indication that they belong to a more matriarchal, a more feminine milieu. Such too, was the clear view of the Midrashim, the commentaries dating back some two thousand years "in an unbroken line from Ezra to the eleventh century (in which) the Holy Writ was preached with the help of legend, parable, story and maxim." (Epstein, p. xviii f)

The Midrash Rabbah on Ruth says of this passage (vol. 8, p. 35), "A heathen indeed has no father," meaning, Hartmann elucidates (p. 16), that "with him the matriarchate rules, and not, as with the Israelites, the patriarchate."

There are a few biblical passages referring to the "mother's house." One is in the above mentioned story about seeking a wife for Isaac. After Rebekah had offered water to Abraham's servant and his camels at the well, and he had made himself known to her, she "ran and told all this to her mother's household." (Gen. 24:28). This helps us understand Abraham's urgency in twice insisting "do not take my son back there!" The other passages are in the Song of Songs, that outspoken love song described in Rivkah Kluger's seminar as "Eros returning to the biblical world as though through the back door." The two passages read:

> Scarcely had I passed them
> When I found the one I love.
> I held him fast, I would not let him go
> Till I brought him to my mother's house,
> To the chamber of her who conceived me.
>
> Songs, 3:4

And a second time:

> If only it could be as with a brother,
> As if you had nursed at my mother's breast:
> Then I could kiss you
> When I met you in the street,
> And no one would despise me.
> I would lead you, I would bring you
> To the house of my mother,
> Of her who taught me –
> I would let you drink of the spiced wine,
> Of my pomegranate juice.
>
> Songs, 8:1f.

The origin of the Song of Songs, in the view of many modern scholars, goes back to the Ishtar cult. Whether or not it is actually what is left of a liturgy for the celebration of the wedding of Ishtar and Tammuz, there is no doubt that many allusions in the Song of Songs refer to elements of the cult of that fertility-love goddess, (Rowley, p. 217ff.) so it is no surprise to find "the mother's house" in so central a role in it.

That Ruth was referred to her mother's house is not because she had no father, as we learn when Boaz tells her that he knows "how you left your father and your mother." Nor is it necessary that the father be alive in order to refer so to his house. His father was long dead when Abraham told his servant to "go to my father's house" for a wife for his son. (Gen. 24:38) Naomi's phraseology in this instance reflects the dominance of the kind of femininity which Ruth and Orpah represent. Their's was the realm of the nature cycle, where the love/mother goddess still played an important, if not a leading role. Their accompanying Naomi was more likely prompted by an adhesion to the mother figure she had come to be for them, than a turning toward her spiritual God Yahweh, who was the antithesis of the mother-dominated male nature god. When she bid them return, they wept

> and said to her, "No, we will return with you to your people."
> But Naomi replied, "Turn back, my daughters! Why should you go with me? Have I any more sons in my body who might be husbands for you? Turn back, my daughters, for I am too old to be married. Even if I thought there was hope for me, even if I were married tonight and I also bore sons, should you wait for them to grow up? Should you on their account debar yourselves from marriage?" (1:10-13)

Here Naomi bids them return a second time, and this time dis-identifies herself from the bounteous nature-mother. She is full of understanding and sympathy for her daughters-in-law and she is also aware of the purely natural feminine needs and desires which she well understands and shares. It is not that she is a "spiritualized" woman in contrast to their pagan earthiness. She is rather that femininity which, having been freed from bondage in Egypt and brought to the revelation at Mt. Sinai, was fated to be subject to a spiritual God, and she accepts that subjection – not without some complaint.

> Oh no, my daughters! My lot is far more bitter than yours, for the hand of the Lord has struck out against me. (1:13)

It is this being subject to a spiritual God which is so bitter for the "natural" woman – to this very day. How accurately and succinctly, in expressing her individual feelings, does Naomi describe the general, collective problem of the feminine, starting in that era when it was, of necessity, (see p. 16 above) suppressed by the newly arisen religion; "the hand of the Lord (Yahweh) has struck out against me," against the feminine element of the Hebrew psyche. (With the spread of Biblical monotheism, this became a problem to all its women adherents. "I am much too bitter for you" is the rendering of two modern scholars, Joüon and Rudolph, if we restore the word "bitter" (Hebrew *mar*) for their substituted "unfortunate" or "unhappy" ("malheureuse" and "unglücklich").

In modern woman the development of the archetypal masculine element in her psyche, i.e., the animus, is experienced in the best case as spiritually creative. Negatively, when not yet integrated, "he" appears tyrannically, or at times, as a demon or an incubus. As Rivkah Kluger demonstrates (1978), the Bible shows this problem in its beginnings, when dealing with the masculine spirit became a necessity for the woman. Previously she had been contained by the feminine principle alone, by the mother, the fertility or love goddess, who originally, as in Ishtar, were one.

Under the goddess creativity belonged to the earth, the body, the female. The male was an appendage thereto, a means therefor, a phallus primarily, whose function was to serve the feminine in both her aspects, fertility and love. The male, the phallus, was a creative instrument, but despite a certain degree of autonomy, he was, in the last analysis, still just a tool in the service of the feminine, which brought him forth, and to which he ever and again returned. This ever recurrent cycle of the birth and death of the god was the hallmark of polytheism with its all-powerful goddess.

With Yahveh the creative principle became a masculine prerogative. Yahweh alone was the Creator, and that through the spirit, not the body. No Great Mother, *mater* (i.e., matter) creating now by means of a male (i.e., phallic) tool, but the masculine spirit alone and unaided, the Word, Logos:

> And God said … … … and it was so. (Gen. 1)

The clash between these two creative principles, the masculine and the feminine, has, at least initially, a disturbing effect on the latter, for the woman. She becomes barren. She is torn out of her containment in the mother-goddess. The restoration of her femininity comes only after a meeting with, or dedication to, the masculine God (R. Kluger, 1978). So the barrenness of Sarah was ended after the visit of God's messengers (Gen. 18:9ff) and that of Hannah when she vowed to dedicate her son to the Lord (1 Sam. 1:9-11).

But relinquishing the support of the goddess, her Self-symbol, was no light task for the woman. It was this subjection of the feminine to the masculine, of eros to logos, which Naomi personified, and which made her "much too bitter" for the polytheistic femininity of Orpah and Ruth. Naomi is a part of, and adheres to, the Yahwistic patriarchy, and returns to her land, yet we can sense her love for the Moabite women and the sacrifice she makes in dismissing them. She must go the new, the patriarchal way, but she sends her daughters-in-law back to their matriarchal pattern in which their natural femininity is more likely to receive fulfillment.

5. The Change in the Feminine

There are two reactions from the side of the feminine:

> They broke into weeping again, and Orpah kissed her mother-in-law farewell. But Ruth clung to her. (1:14)

When Naomi first bids them return, both women refuse. But when she makes clear that she is not the fruitful feminine ("Have I any more sons in my body who might be husbands for you?"), Orpah turns back. The Septuagint here adds "and returned to her people."

The name Orpah comes from *oreph*, which means "mane," "neck," "back of the neck." *Oreph* is frequently used in the sense of turning back before something, as in Jeremiah, where God speaks of the backsliding leaders,

> They say to wood, "You are my father,"
> To stone, "You gave birth to me,"
> While to Me they turn their backs (*oreph*)
> And not their faces.
>
> Jer. 2:27

The Midrash Ruth Rabbah (ii:9, p. 31) explains that her name was Orpah "because she turned her back on her mother-in-law."

The name Ruth, often derived from *re'uth*, "friendship," which in turn comes from the root *ro'eh*, "comrade," whose derivatives include such words as "yoke," "wedding," "bridegroom" and "bride," is widely disputed because of philological difficulties, and is not generally acceptable. But the Akkadian word *Ruttum* or *Rutum*, also meaning "friendship," is the probable root, according to Prof. Aaron Shaffer of the Department of Assyriology of the Hebrew University, to whom I am indebted for this information, and poses no philological problem.

Ruth and Orpah are both representatives of the same pagan femininity. Legend (Ginzberg, iv:31) makes them sisters and confirms their importance as symbols for a ruling principle by seeing them as princesses, daughters of the Moabite king Eglon (Judges, 3:12-30.) We see here a split or a differentiation in the pagan feminine principle. One part, of its own accord, attaches itself to the newer, patriarchal line of developing consciousness. The other returns to its old path and disappears from view, i.e., returns to the unconscious which matriarchy or paganism was for the Hebrews.

The motif of the double figure is frequent in psychic processes, and ranges from identical pairs to complete opposites. On a personal level, as in dreams, the appearance of a double figure may refer to the two aspects or qualities of a content, one being more adapted or conscious, the other less adapted or more instinctive. Or the doubling may indicate that some heretofore unconscious content is approaching consciousness, and is being separated into its two opposite aspects. Differentiation is always a primary step for consciousness (Jung, C. W. 12, par. 30, 398). Often enough only one part is assimilable, and the other falls back into the unconscious. On a mythological level we have such pairs as Cain and Abel, Gilgamesh and Enkidu, Jacob and Esau, Castor and Pollux, and also the two goats in the scapegoat ritual.

In our story, one part of the pagan femininity clings to Naomi, while the other part leaves her, with fateful consequences according to legend (Ginzberg, iv, p. 86), which sees Goliath as a descendant of Orpah. This legend nicely amplifies the archetypal viewpoint, for Goliath was the giant-champion of the Philistines who were always encroaching on the Israelites' newly won and precariously held territory. David, descended from Ruth, was the hero who slew him. Psychologically this is a picture of the victory over the giant forces of the unconscious which are always threatening to recapture the areas, originally unconscious, which the much younger growing consciousness has won for itself. Or to retake those parts which are impelled to attach to it, as Ruth clings to Naomi, who, a third time, urges her to return.

"See, your sister-in-law has returned to her people and her gods. Go, follow your sister-in-law." But Ruth replied, "Do not urge me to leave you, to turn back and not follow you. For wherever you go, I will go; wherever you lodge, I will lodge; your people shall be my people, and your God my God. Where you die, I will die, and there will I be buried. Thus and more may the Lord do to me if anything but death parts me from you." (1:15-17)

What the ultimate issue was is clear: a choice of gods. Naomi urges Ruth to return, like Orpah did, "to her people and to her gods." Ruth's famous reply is one of passionate devotion, a comprehensive adoption of all that pertains to Naomi. It is virtually an identification with her. Naomi's repeated attempts to send her back were really a test of her determination, even if not so intended. Naomi had to make abundantly clear to Ruth what, or how little, there was to look forward to by remaining with her. Ruth's decision, if it were to be meaningful, had to be a conscious decision. In effect she was deciding to adhere not only to Naomi, but to her God. This point, clear from the text alone, receives emphasis in a Midrashic legend (Ruth R. ii, 22, pp. 39f) where Ruth's declaration is expanded into a dialogue in which Naomi expounds the burden which the Hebrew religion would be for her. In a feminine way, by a devoted attachment, Ruth accepted the heroic task of moving towards increasing consciousness. The steadfastness of the hero is often tested and he must be aware of what he is doing. So, for example, were attempts made to deter Gilgamesh from going a new way. Gilgamesh, king of Uruk, wanted to go forth to kill the giant Humbaba who guarded the cedar forest, the realm of the mother. The elders of Uruk tried to dissuade him, saying:

Thou art young, O Gilgamesh, and thy heart has carried thee away. Thou dost not know what thou proposest to do.

(Tabl. III, col. v, lines 190f.)

David was similarly discouraged by Saul when he offered to fight Goliath.

But Saul said to David, "You cannot go to that Philistine and fight him; you are only a boy, and he has been a warrior from his youth!" (1 Sam. 17:33)

But Gilgamesh and David persisted in their intentions, with the result that the elders, and Saul, respectively, ceased their objections and blessed them. Ruth too, persisted, and won her way.

When [Naomi] saw how determined she was to go with her, she ceased to argue with her, and they two went on until they reached Bethlehem. (1:18f.)

Ruth began her new life in Bethlehem, that city on the way to which, in an earlier day, the most feminine of the mothers of Israel died (Gen. 35:19), Rachel, who according to legend and popular belief, intercedes in heaven for her children, as seen in Jeremiah 31:14 – "A cry is heard in Ramah.... Rachel weeping for her children."

Rachel died *on the way*, which has its symbolic meaning. It will be recalled that she stole her father's teraphim, household gods (Gen. 31:19), when Jacob hurriedly left Laban's house. She took her old gods with her when accompanying Jacob on the way Yahweh had sent him. That is why she died so early, according to legend, for Jacob had said to Laban who came looking for his teraphim, "anyone with whom you find your gods shall not remain alive!" (Gen. 31:32) Rachel died "on the way." She did not quite make the transition from the old gods to the new God. She was buried on the road to Ephrath – now Bethlehem. (Gen. 35:19) But Ruth and Naomi arrived there.

When they arrived in Bethlehem, the whole city buzzed with excitement over them. The women said, "Can this be Naomi?" "Do not call me Naomi,"[18] she replied. "Call me Mara,[19] for Shaddai[20] has made my lot very bitter. I went away full, and the

---

[18] Pleasantness
[19] Bitterness
[20] Usually rendered "the Almighty."

Lord has brought me back empty. How can you call me Naomi, when the Lord has dealt harshly with me, when Shaddai has brought misfortune upon me!" (1:19-21)

Naomi's words here, as in her earlier complaint about her state (p. 31), are like a reflection of the fate of the collective feminine principle, expressed in an individual case. The feminine element is emphasized in this scene, in which the conversation takes place between Naomi and the women of the city. Grief, especially over the death of her children, has a special nuance for a woman, who is literally filled by them before their birth. This is a woman's mystery which women alone can fully understand.

The women hardly recognize Naomi after her long absence, because of the great change, the loss of her husband and sons, which she bewails with particular reference to her emptiness. It is perhaps a mark of the devaluation of the woman in the society, that Naomi apparently takes no notice of her acquisition of Ruth, who so recently gave voice to a rarity of devotion difficult to ignore. It is not only the loss of the men, but also the addition of Ruth, which means a change for Naomi. The change in the nature of the feminine due to the entrance of Ruth can well be seen in a legend.

> The wife of Boaz died on that day, and all Israel assembled to pay their respects, and just then Ruth entered with Naomi. Thus one was taken out when the other entered, and "All the city was astir concerning them, and the women said: 'Is this Naomi?'"
>
> Midrash Ruth Rabbah, iii. 6, p. 47

This brief legend, symbolically seen, condenses the events to their psychological meaning. With the return of Naomi and Ruth from Moab, a previous form of Hebrew femininity died. "And just then Ruth entered...." *Ruth* entered. And this caused a change in Naomi, wherefore the women asked "Is this Naomi?" The patriarchal femininity had undergone a change, an addition from the pagan world, an enrichment, and was destined to bear a new fruit.

Thus Naomi returned from the country of Moab; she returned with her daughter-in-law, Ruth the Moabite. They arrived in Bethlehem at the beginning of the barley harvest. (1:22)

Chapter Two

1. The Re-appearance of the Masculine

Chapter one opened with a famine in the land, and closed with a harvest. At the beginning we were introduced to a certain "man of Bethlehem," Elimelech, and his family, a totality. We saw the gradual disappearance of the masculine components of this family, and the addition of a new feminine element. The chapter ended in an entirely feminine scene – the confrontation between the newly arrived Ruth and Naomi, and the women of Bethlehem, among whom they now took their place.

Chapter two begins with the introduction of a new but related masculine element, Boaz.

> Now Naomi had a kinsman on her husband's side, a man of substance, of the family of Elimelech, whose name was Boaz.
>
> (2:1)

Boaz's relationship to Elimelech is mentioned twice in this sentence. In the next verse but one, we again read: "Boaz, who was of Elimelech's family." It is emphasized that Boaz is kin to Elimelech, whose name, we recall, means "my God is king." Thus it is the same Yahwistic stock which he represents. The vitality of this Boaz, who is linked to the masculine component of our original quaternity, is specifically indicated by his characterization as *gibbor chayil*, "a man of substance." This phrase is used in the Bible to designate a courageous warrior (as of David, cf. 1 Sam. 16:18), and also men of outstanding note, virtue, and wealth.[21] The Hebrew word *chayil,* "valor" also means "bravery," "strength," "right-heartedness," "virtue." This word is used to describe Ruth (3:11), there translated as "a virtuous woman."

His name too, gives indication of the vitality of this new representative of spiritual masculinity. Boaz means "in him is strength," according to most commentators, and this is also the traditional interpretation (Ruth R., p. 81). Of all the names in the Book of Ruth, Boaz is the only one which appears in another connection in the Bible, a connection which is meaningful for our story. Boaz is the name of the left of the two pillars which stood before the temple.

In view of the great detail with which they are described[22], these free-standing pillars, which had no structural function, must have been of considerable importance. Their names were *Jachin,* "He will establish," and *Boaz,* "in Him is strength," and the traditional view is that they bore testimony to the might of God. W. Robertson Smith, in his *Religion of the Semites,* thinks "they were doubtless symbols of Jehovah." (p. 208, n. 1) This is disputed on the grounds that there is no intimation of this in the Bible. However we do find many such usages in the pagan world.

Two pillars stood before many temples in ancient Phoenicia, Syria, Cyprus,[23] Babylonia,[24] and in Egypt. The two pillars before the temples in Paphos and Hieropolis stood for the diety, and the god Melkarth was worshipped at Tyre in the form of two pillars, as Smith notes in this connection.

Clearly the pillars in the surrounding world, if not in Israel, were gods. In the myth of Adapa, the gate of Anu was guarded

---

[21] Cf. 1 Sam. 9:1, 2 KIngs, 15:20, Neh. 11:14.

[22] 1 Kings, 7:15ff., Jer. 52:17ff., 2 Chron. 3:16f., 4:12f.

[23] R. B. Y. Scott, "The Pillars Jachin and Boaz," Jl. of Bibl. Lit., 1939, **58**, p. 143; W. F. Albright, *Archeology and Religion of Israel,* 1946, p. 144.

[24] Sir L. Woolley, *The Sumerians,* p. 40, cited by Staples, p. 151.

by Tammuz and Gishzida. Staples (p. 152), in connecting these two gods with the two pillars guarding temple gates, uses this myth to support his argument for equating Boaz with Tammuz. Gressmann goes so far as to emend the name of the pillar from Boaz to Ba'al, the Canaanite god.[25]

It is not difficult to see a glimmering of the myths of dying and resurrected Tammuz, Osiris, etc., behind this point of our story. In the beginning we saw famine, departure to a strange land, and Elimelech's death; and now we see harvest in his own land, and the appearance of a strong figure, of the family of Elimelech. Similarly in the "seasonal" myths we find the death of vegetation, the death of the god, and his descent to the underworld, followed after a period of time by his resurrection or revitalization, and return to earth, which is once again fruitful. A very significant difference however, is that the events in our story take place entirely in the world of man. The archetypes are that much closer to being "*realized*" instead of endlessly recurring only in the unreachable realm of the gods. Regardless of his symbolical meaning or divine parallels, Boaz in our story appears as a human being. Just at this point in Ruth Rabbah (p. 51) there is an illuminating comment comparing the Hebrew word order in which Boaz is introduced in the text, with similar word orders in other Biblical passages. The Midrash says that this particular word order is found only in the cases of righteous men, "because *they are like their Creator.*"

2. The Meeting Between the Masculine and the Feminine

Now that Boaz has been introduced as an important personality, the reader expects a meeting between him and

---

[25] H. Gressmann, "Dolmen, Masseben und Mapflöcher," in Z. A. W. vol. 29, 1909, p. 122.

Ruth, and wonders how this will come about and what will be
its effect.

> Ruth the Moabitess said to Naomi, "I would like to go to the
> fields and glean among the ears of grain, behind someone who
> may show me kindness." "Yes, daughter, go," she replied; and off
> she went. She came and gleaned in a field, behind the reapers;
> and, as luck would have it, it was the piece of land belonging to
> Boaz, who was of Elimelech's family. (2:2, 3)

True to her declaration in the first chapter, Ruth's words
and action portray devotion and submission to Naomi, and a
willingness, or eagerness, to care for her. Though it is
described as a fortuitous occurrence, there is a feeling of divine
providence in her "happening" to light on Boaz's field, particularly since it is pointed out again that he belongs to the family
of Elimelech. Legend even tells us that an angel led Ruth to
Boaz's field.

> Presently Boaz arrived from Bethlehem. He greeted the reapers,
> "The Lord be with you!" And they responded, "The Lord bless
> you!" Boaz said to the servant who was in charge of the reapers,
> "Whose girl is that?" The servant in charge of the reapers replied,
> "She is a Moabite girl who came back with Naomi from the
> country of Moab. She said, 'Please let me glean and gather
> among the sheaves behind the reapers.' She has been on her feet
> ever since she came this morning. She has rested but little in the
> hut." (2:4-7)

Boaz's proprietorship is here pictured. He is a leading
figure, an authority, a symbol of the ruling patriarchal element. The form of his greeting, "The Lord (literally Yahweh)
be with you," sets the sign under which he lives. In contrast,
Ruth's foreignness is accented, associated however, with her
loyalty to Naomi. Boaz takes cognizance of Ruth's presence at
once. His interest in her is immediate and positive, and
increases throughout the chapter.

> Boaz said to Ruth, "Listen to me, daughter. Don't go to glean in
> another field. Don't go elsewhere, but stay here close to my girls.

Keep your eyes on the field they are reaping, and follow them. I have ordered the men not to molest you. And when you are thirsty, go to the jars and drink some of [the water] that the men have drawn." (2:8, 9)

Later he invites her to join the meal, gives her enough so that she has some left to take home to Naomi, and he even instructs his men to "pull some [stalks] out of the heaps and leave them for her...." This foreign woman who appears in his field, humbly asking permission to glean, and industriously pursuing her lowly task, excites a remarkably warm response in Boaz. Though his feelings are properly paternal in their expression, a hint of more than paternal interest can be discerned. His concern for her goes beyond what one would expect of a kindly disposed landowner toward a poor gleaner. She not only may glean in his field, he insists that she remain *only* there. She is no young girl (legend puts her at 40) yet he is anxious that she stick close to his women. (The Hebrew text has the same word as was used when Ruth "clung" to Naomi, here translated "stay close to.") This seems to be a further precaution, since he also charged the young men not to molest her. The word *noga*, "touch," "reach," "molest," can also be used in a more specific sense, as in Proverbs 6:29:

It is the same with one who sleeps with his fellow's wife;
None who touches her will go unpunished.

That Boaz's feelings are not merely paternal is proved by his words when she comes to him during the night, later, at the threshing floor. He blesses her for "your latest deed of loyalty is greater than the first, in that you have not turned to younger men, whether poor or rich" (the first loyalty referring to her return with Naomi). (3:10)

But what is it that makes Ruth produce this effect on Boaz? It is eros which evokes such warmth. Through Boaz's reaction to Ruth we can almost sense the unseen presence of a love god – or goddess. There is no indication in the story that it was Ruth's beauty which impelled Boaz to be so attentive. At least it is not mentioned. Legend indeed, remarks on it, telling us that "she was of such extraordinary beauty that no man could look at her without becoming passionately enamored of her." (Ginzberg, vi, p. 192) This sounds more like the attribute of a goddess than of a mortal. In a later Kabbalistic work, the Zohar Ruth, Ruth's name is interpreted by a play on its letters to mean "dove," and this again reminds us of the goddess of love, whose bird was the dove. There are still other threads linking Ruth to an Ishtar or Aphrodite-like figure.

An especially illuminating legend in this connection (Ginzberg, iii, p. 351) tells us that Moses wanted to war on the descendants of Lot after the episode at Shittim (see above, p. 22 ff). God forbade this saying that the two nations must be spared because two doves were to spring from them: the Moabitess Ruth, and the Ammonitess Naamah. (This was the wife of Solomon, the mother of Rehoboam. Cf. 1 Kings, 14:21.) One version of this legend has God say that He "lost something valuable among them." (Ginzberg, v. iii, p. 406). The idea that God "lost something" among Lot's descendants, and so must spare them until He regains it at a later date, is really a daring thought. Yet it fits exactly with the present thesis as to the meaning of the Book of Ruth, and shows that legends, coming from the unconscious as do myths, have an "understanding" of their archetypal meaning.

This "lost something" is a particular aspect of femininity. Until it is restored, something, obviously, will be missing. As was already shown in Rivkah Kluger's paper "Old Testament Roots of Woman's Spiritual Problem," this loss was necessary at the time in order to permit the firm establishment of the masculine upward striving sun principle. There was the danger that this new step in consciousness could succumb to the negative power of the goddess. We have only to recall how Ishtar crippled her lovers and transformed them into animals, what she herself calls "My stinking deeds and my rotten acts" (Heidel, pp. 51f.), though with no sign of remorse. But only when this "lost" aspect of femininity is found again, and redeemed, will wholeness be restored.

3. The Inner Purpose of the Meeting

The tendency toward achieving wholeness, a balanced totality, here requiring the redemption of the lost value which had become strange and foreign, this archetypal tendency, underlies the response which Ruth evoked in Boaz. The need for uniting with the opposite, for attaining wholeness, existed in both of them. It was Ruth's need which unconsciously led her to cleave to Naomi, to go with her to Judah, to find Boaz's plot, and to get nourishment from his values, i.e., "to glean in his field, and drink of his water," as he charges her to do. So too, the Midrashim[26], which interpret her gleaning as following God's teaching, and the water as the Holy Spirit. They refer to Isaiah 12:3; "… water out of the wells of salvation."

> She prostrated herself with her face to the ground, and said to him, "Why are you so kind as to single me out[27], when I am a foreigner?" (2:10)

Such obeisance, as Staples points out,[28] is given in the Bible only to God, a king, or a prophet. It reflects, therefore, the degree of spiritual value which Boaz represents for Ruth. Again, as is inevitable in translations, there is a certain amount of dilution of the connotations present in the original. Joüon (p. 51) points out that the Hebrew *hikir*, "take cognizance of," implies a more active attitude than the English generally conveys. It contains the feeling of "pay attention to," "regard attentively"; and the word *nochriyah*, "foreigner" (R. V. "stranger"), more properly means "unknown." The Hebrew

---

[26] Hartmann, pp. 39 ff.
[27] others, more literally, "to take cognizance/notice of me"
[28] Staples, p. 152; cf. 1 Kings 1:16, 2 Kings 4:37, Neh. 8:6.

text brings out a little more clearly the intensity of Boaz's interest, and the "unknownness" of Ruth.

Boaz's answer lauds her virtue, but it tells us more besides.

> Boaz said in reply, "I have been told of all that you did for your mother-in-law after the death of your husband, how you left your father and mother and the land of your birth and came to a people you had not known before. May the Lord *reward* your deeds. May you have a *full recompense* from the Lord, the God of Israel, under whose wings you have sought refuge!" (2:11, 12)

The words "reward," *shalem*, and "*full* recompense," *shalemah*, are intimately related, as can be seen from the transliteration of the Hebrew. They both come from the same root, whose meaning includes: "to be complete," "to make whole," "give back," "*integrum esse.*"

Wholeness, healing, completeness, are all in the root *shlm*, whence its sense of reconstituting, repaying, recompensing, making full, making sound. Thus it is possible in reading verse 11 to hear as undertone "May the Lord make whole your deeds. May you have wholeness from the Lord...." As we shall see, Ruth was "recompensed," did in fact receive a "full reward," a reward of "being made whole," and that at the hand of Boaz. A complete reward, a reward of being made whole, is in effect nothing less than redemption. This we can see in Isaiah 62:11, 12;

> See, the Lord has proclaimed
> To the end of the earth:
> Announce to Fair Zion,
> Your Deliverer is coming!
> See, his *reward* (*sachar*) is with Him,
> His *recompense* (*pe'ullah*) before Him.

> And they shall be called, "The Holy people,
> The *Redeemed* (*ge'ulai*) of the Lord,"
> And you shall be called, "Sought Out,
> A City Not Forsaken."

To anticipate briefly here: the word "redeemed," above, is a form of the Hebrew *go'el*, which we shall deal with at some length later. Suffice it now to remark that the whole point of our story hinges on the fact that Boaz, by virtue of being a kinsman of Elimelech, which devolved certain duties upon him, was the *go'el*, the "redeemer," of Ruth.

Boaz says: "May you have a full recompense (wholeness) from the Lord, the God of Israel, *under whose wings you have sought* refuge." It is noteworthy that in a later passage Ruth uses the same figure of speech, asking Boaz to 'spread his wing over her.' This occurs in the scene at the threshing floor, where she says: "I am your handmaid Ruth. Spread your robe over your handmaid, for you are a *go'el*.'" (3:9) The English translation has "redeeming kinsman" for *go'el*, and this will be discussed later. The phrase "spread your robe" is literally "spread your *wing*" in Hebrew. This metaphor is used as a symbol of marriage, and the actual practice has parallels in Arabic customs maintained into modern times.[29] The same metaphor also occurs in Ezekiel 16:8, in a passage which is significant for our story. There God, speaking to Jerusalem personified as a woman, says:

> I passed by you and saw that your time for love had arrived. So I spread my robe (literally wing) over you and covered your nakedness, and I entered into a covenant with you by oath – declares the Lord God – thus you became Mine.

The relationship between God and Israel is frequently depicted as a marriage,[30] and God is also often referred to as the *go'el*, the Redeemer, of Israel.

In the light of all the above, Boaz's speech to Ruth (2:11, 12; see p. 46 above) has important undertones, and foreshad-

[29] R. Patai, *Sex and Family in the Bible and the Middle East*, Doubleday Co., New York, 1950.

[30] cf. R. Kluger, "The Image of Marriage between God and Israel as it Occurs in the Prophets of the Old Testament, especially Ezekiel XVI." Spring, New York, 1950, pp. 70-89.

ows all the further development. It also shows, by how highly
it is valued, what a great and difficult step this was for Ruth,
the step from Moab to Israel, from matriarchy to patriarchy.
Ruth is grateful for his words.

> She answered, "You are most kind, my lord, to comfort me and
> to speak gently to your maidservant – though I am not so much
> as one of your maidservants." (2:13)

We remarked above that underlying Boaz's concern for
Ruth was the urge to redeem a lost value which had become
strange and foreign. Ruth's response acknowledges this, her
foreignness, and indicates a comparable desire on her part to
be accepted. Yet her words are not just a humble acquiescence.
They give notice that accepting her will not be on terms of an
identification with the then present status of the feminine.
The Hebrew *lo ehyeh* means not merely "I am not" (as one of
your maidservants) but also "I do not wish to be,"[31] as we find
it used in Isaiah 3:7: "I will not be a dresser of wounds."
Legend (Ruth R. p. 61) takes cognizance of this meaning by
having Boaz answer her that she is not as one of his maidservants, but as one of the mothers of Israel. Since the four
Matriarchs (Sarah, Rebekah, Rachel and Leah) are idealized
types of womanhood, this in effect would make Ruth a new
"ideal feminine" type.

Following this, Boaz takes another step in accepting Ruth
as a part of the community.

> At mealtime, Boaz said to her, "Come over here and partake of
> the meal, and dip your morsel in the vinegar." So she sat down
> beside the reapers. He handed her roasted grain, and she ate her
> fill and had some left over. (2:14)

Eating together is a form of communion. Ruth is becoming
integrated into the community, as is also hinted at by the
phrase "she sat beside the reapers," although Yair Zakovitch,

---

[31] Joüon, p. 57.

in his very detailed commentary, emphasizes (p. 78) that in her modesty she sat "beside" the reapers, and not among them. The Hebrew word *wayyitsbat*, he "handed" (her), occurs no place else in the Bible. From its Akkadian and Ugaritic roots, it is related to the word *tsebet*, "pliers" or "tongs," and in this instance it describes the roasting of grain over a fire, as is done to this day by Arab reapers in the field. Thus Boaz himself roasted the grain which he then offered her. As Zakovitch observes, by this action Boaz expresses a greater closeness to Ruth than was expressed by his words. This nourishment which she receives at the hands of the masculine "satisfies" Ruth, "who ate her fill," with enough left for Naomi too, as we see later, when "she took out and gave her what she had left over after eating her fill." (2:18). With the advent of Ruth, some special consideration is being paid to the needy feminine.

> When she got up again to glean, Boaz gave orders to his workers, "You are not only to let her glean among the sheaves, without interference, but you must also pull some [stalks] out of the heaps and leave them for her to glean, and not scold her."
> She gleaned in the field until evening. Then she beat out what she had gleaned – it was about an *ephah* of barley. (2:15-17)

Seen symbolically, this no longer represents a repression of the feminine. She no longer is kept at a distance, but may glean right among the sheaves; she is not to be scolded nor interfered with; moreover, she is no longer dependent on lean remnants, but is quietly supplied from the main crop. An *ephah* is between 15 and 25 kilograms, which is much more than "gleaning." Ruth returns well laden to Naomi.

> ... and carried it back with her to the town. When her mother-in-law saw what she had gleaned, and when she also took out and gave her what she had left over after eating her fill, her mother-in-law asked her, "Where did you glean today? Where did you work? Blessed be he who took such generous notice of you!" (2:18f.)

As we already remarked, Naomi is the immediate benefi-
ciary of Ruth's gains. She sees the abundance of Ruth's
gleanings, and blesses him who "took such generous notice" of
her. This is the same word *hikir* as is rendered "to single out"
in verse 10. The blessing falls on him who "paid attention" to
Ruth.

> So she told her mother-in-law whom she had worked with,
> saying, "The name of the man with whom I worked today is
> Boaz."
> Naomi said unto her daughter-in-law, "Blessed be he of the Lord,
> who has not failed in His kindness to the living or to the dead!
> For," Naomi explained to her daughter-in-law, "the man is
> related to us, he is one of our redeeming kinsman." (2:19, 20)

Learning his name, Naomi tells Ruth that Boaz is *karov*,
"related," (or, R. S. V., "near of kin"), and realizes therefore
that he is their *go'el*, here translated as "redeeming kinsman"
(R. S. V. "nearest kin"). For a proper understanding of the
Book of Ruth it is necessary to know some of the implications,
the rights and duties, pertaining to kinship among the
Hebrews. That Naomi blesses the Lord for His kindness to the
living and *to the dead*, is an allusion to the levirate marriage
(from the Latin *levir*, "a husband's brother").

4. Levirate Marriage

If a man died childless it was the duty of the next-of-kin to
marry the widow in order to raise a son and heir to the dead,
"that his name may not be blotted out in Israel." The law of
levirate marriage (Deut. 25:5ff.) limits this duty to the brother
of the deceased, but there is evidence that this is a limitation
of an obligation which in earlier times devolved also on farther
removed relatives, in the order of the nearness of kinship.

This is to be seen for example in the story of Tamar and
Judah (Gen. 38). Judah's eldest son, Er, husband of Tamar,

died childless. And Judah said (v. 8) to Onan (his second son):
"Join with your brother's wife and do your duty by her as a
brother-in-law, and provide offspring for your brother." Onan
spilled his seed on the ground rather than give it for his
brother, wherefore God slew him. Judah then bade Tamar to
wait until his third son, Shelah, were grown up. Time passed,
and Shelah being withheld from Tamar, she veiled herself, and
sat at the roadside waiting for Judah to pass. Judah, mistaking
her for a harlot, himself unwittingly performed the duty of
raising a seed for the dead. When Tamar was later accused of
harlotry, she proved by the pledges she had earlier demanded
from Judah, that he was the one who had made her pregnant,
and Judah acknowledged her virtue, saying (v. 26), "She is
more in the right than I; inasmuch as I did not give her to my
son Shelah."

From this we can deduce that the law on levirate marriage
as written in Deuteronomy (which is one of the later Biblical
texts) represents a narrowing of an earlier, broader practice,
where the responsibility for raising an heir to the dead was not
limited to the brother alone, but extended to a wider circle of
kinship. Now we can understand why Naomi, hearing that
Ruth had gleaned on the field of Boaz, and recognizing that
he was their kinsman, praised God for not leaving off His
kindness "to the living and to the dead." What naturally came
to her mind was this duty, which would mean a husband for
Ruth (the kindness to the living) and a seed for Mahlon, and
hence also for Elimelech, "that his name may not be blotted
out" (the kindness to the dead). This was to be seen from her
very next sentence: "The man is related to us; he is our
redeeming kinsman."

5. The Meanings of *Go'el*

As already remarked, the word translated here as "redeeming kinsman," is *go'el*. The noun *go'el*, from the verb *ga'al*

meaning "to redeem," "to re-vindicate," "to buy back," is a term applied to that kinsman upon whom certain redemptive duties fall. Thus, if because of impoverishment a man sold himself into servitude,

> "… he shall have the right of *redemption* even after he has given himself over. One of his kinsmen (literally, brothers) shall *redeem* him, or his uncle, or his uncle's son, shall *redeem* him, or anyone of his family who is of his own flesh shall *redeem* him; or if he prospers, he may *redeem* himself."
>
> Lev. 25:48 f.

(The italicized words are forms of *ga'al.*) In this passage we can see how the obligation passes from nearest to more distant kinsmen, as was probably the case with levirate marriage in earlier times.

Not only the person of the kinsman, but also his land which had been sold, had a claim to redemption. In the law covering this eventuality, we find the term *go'el,* "redeemer," applied to the kinsman who was liable to this obligation. In our scholarly New JPS (1962) translation, the term is accurately given as "redeemer," but in other translations, including the R. S. V. it is rendered "kin" or "kinsman."

> If your kinsman (literally "brother") is in straits and has to sell part of his holding, his nearest *redeemer (go'el)* (others, kinsman) shall come, and *redeem (ga'al)* what his kinsman (literally brother) has sold.
>
> Lev. 25:25

A third duty toward one's "flesh and blood" was that of vindicating the murder of a kinsman. The kinsman who fulfills this obligation is called the "*go'el* of blood," rendered in most traditional English translations as the "avenger of blood."

> The blood-avenger himself shall put the murderer to death.
>
> Numb. 35:19

Since these duties of *ge'ullah*, of redemption and vindication, were incumbent on the nearest kinsman (in turn – cf. Lev. 25:48f cited above), the term *go'el* took on, by extension, the meaning of "near kinsman." Hence it is that in a number of translations of the Bible, including most of the English ones, the noun *go'el* in the Book of Ruth is given as "near kinsman," and the verb *ga'al* is sometimes rendered "to do the part of a kinsman" (where the object is a person, i.e. Ruth), and sometimes, more properly, "to redeem" (where the object is a piece of land, as in chapter four). German translations use "Löser" where *go'el* refers to man, and "Erlöser" where it applies to God. English has no such distinction for the word 'redeemer' in its divine and profane usages, nor, for that matter, is any distinction made in the Hebrew; *go'el* is used both for God and man.

If, however, we understand *go'el* merely as a near kinsman, especially in the Book of Ruth, we miss the point. But are we justified in seeing a deeper meaning in it? A further examination of the functions of the *go'el*, and of the occurrences of the word in the Bible, will show the significance of its connotations.

The duties of the *go'el* towards his kinsman, and particularly the practice of levirate marriage, points to a unitary group conception which H. Wheeler Robinson[32] describes as a "corporate personality," in which the unity of the group was expressed as a common blood tie, real or fictitious (as by a blood covenant) and which extended throughout the whole house of Israel. So, for example, when David was elected to kingship,

> All the tribes of Israel came to David at Hebron and said,
> *"We are your own flesh and blood."*
>
> 2 Sam. 5:1

---

[32] H. Wheeler Robinson, "The Hebrew Conception of Corporate Personality," in B. Z. A. W., 1936, 66, pp. 49-62.

Kinship, then, extended beyond the borders of the immediate household, and "wherever such kinship was recognized there was the further recognition of a psychical whole," as A. R. Johnson observes in his work on the root meaning of the word *go'el*.[33]

The community, according to Robinson, was conceived of as a "great ego." This would perhaps be akin to, but far from identical with the mutual identification of the primitives, their *participation mystique* with the tribe or clan; for, as he shows, there developed in Israel a new emphasis of the individual. "In Israel, through the generations, there is an interplay of sociality and individuality.... the individualizing development taking place within the matrix of a social relation to God." The kin group, all of whose members, individually and collectively, had a covenant with God, was a unit whose integrity was vital, and all the duties of the *go'el* are aimed at preserving this integrity.

Heirless death, loss of freedom or of possession, and murder, all constitute a breach of continuity and a disturbance of order and wholeness in the life of the group, as well as of the individual, and it is the function of the *go'el* to restore the lost vitality of the kin-group, and keep intact its essential unity or integrity (Johnson).

The responsibility to redeem the loss or heal the breach in the life of the group, would most naturally fall first to the nearest of kin, and failing his ability to act, go on to the next in line. The one whose task it is to restore or re-vindicate, by this action restores the integrity of the group, redeems its unity, and hence is the *go'el*, the redeemer. That the *go'el* was in practice a kinsman, is obvious. But it is equally clear that, in being called by this term, the *go'el* is primarily distinguished by the function he fulfills, rather than by the mere fact of

---

[33] A. R. Johnson, "The Primary Meaning of "Go'el," in *Supplements to Vetus Testamentum*, Leiden, 1953.

familial relatedness. The function of the *go'el* aims at restoring an equilibrium which has been upset.

The meaning of restoration is also implicit in the term *go'el.* It has a different quality than another Hebrew word which is also translated as "redeem," namely *padah*. Comparing the two words, Driver, in his commentary on Deuteronomy[34] says: "In its technical sense *padah* means *to ransom* a person, or animal, from death, either by a substitute, or by paying a sum of money.... The primary sense of the synonym *go'el* is properly *to resume a claim or right* which has lapsed, *to reclaim, re-vindicate.*"

This sense of reclaiming points up the restorative nature of *ge'ullah*, "redemption." The *go'el* restores balance and harmony to the kin-group as a whole, and thereby to the individuals who are contained in it. To make whole, to establish order, as Jung has shown, is an inherent psychic instinct. A loss of psychic equilibrium, is followed, he points out by "the automatic and instinctive activity of the unconscious, which is aiming all the time at the creation of a new balance...." (CW 7, par. 253) This activity often finds abstract expression in the rounded symbol of the *mandala,* (the Sanskrit term which has come into common parlance since Jung's elucidation of it). "These images ... indicate the possibility of order in wholeness." (CW 16, par. 536)

Not only wholeness, but protection is also a feature of the mandala – "The round or square enclosures ... have the purpose of protective walls...." (CW 11, par. 156). In Johnson's very interesting paper (pp. 72-75) he deduces that protection is a basic meaning of *go'el.* He arrives at this conclusion by first linking the root *go'el* which we have been discussing, with another root *go'el* which has the meaning "defilement," "pollution," related to a verb *ga'al* meaning "to abhor." For example, in Isaiah 59:3: "For your hands are

---

[34] S. R. Driver, "Deuteronomy," *The International Critical Commentary*, Edinburgh, 1902, p. 101.

defiled with blood …," and in Zephaniah 3:1: "Ah, sullied, *polluted,* overbearing city." He argues that both forms of *go'el* derive from a single original primary root meaning "to cover," which, by a process of semantic polarization came to be used in two opposite senses. In the one case, the picture of something "covered with dirt" or anything else abhorrent or offensive, led to the meaning of defilement. In the second case, the image of being covered in a protective sense, as the *go'el* Boaz protects Ruth by symbolically covering her with his skirt (mantle), taking her "under his wing," led to the meaning of protection.

There is no doubt that protection is an element of wholeness, of redemption. We find it in the protective wall of the mandala, and we also see it in the use of the Hebrew *ga'al* in the prayer in Psalm 69:

> 15. Rescue me from the mire;
> let me not sink;
> Let me be rescued from my enemies, and from the watery depths.
> 19. Come near to me and redeem (ga'al) me;
> free (padah) me from my enemies.
>
> Ps. 69:15, 19

and in Proverbs 23:10f, where God acts as the powerful protector of the fatherless, fulfilling the task assigned to the next of kin:

> Do not remove ancient boundary stone;
> Do not encroach upon the field of orphans,
> For they have a mighty Kinsman, (*Go'el)*
> And He will surely take up their cause with you.

Not only is the *go'el* the kinsman who restores and makes whole, but as Heidel points out (p. 212), "… the real *go'el* in the Old Testament is God Himself.… Wherever the verb *ga'al* appears in the psalter or the prophets, God … is the cause of the redemption." As, for example, in Isaiah 47:4:

Our Redeemer (*go'alenu*) – Lord of Hosts is His name –
Is the Holy One of Israel.

Nor is the use of *go'el* in this sense limited to the Psalms and
Prophets. An examination of the word in all its forms (as listed
in the Koehler-Baumgartner Lexicon, which gives all the
occurrences of the words in the Bible), reveals that, not
counting the Book of Ruth, it appears in 22 books of the
Hebrew Bible.[35] In the sense of "redeem" or "Redeemer,"
linked with God, it is widely scattered in the texts and occurs
most often in this connection – in some 34 passages, whereas
with reference to redeeming land, or a person sold into
servitude, it occurs in only three passages, and as avenger of
blood, in only four. It appears nine times in the sense of defile.

We first meet the term in one of the earliest texts, where
Jacob blesses Joseph's sons, and it is already then a divine
activity.

The God who has been my shepherd from my birth to this day –
The Angel who has *redeemed* me from all harm –
Bless the lads.

Gen. 48:15

It occurs in the famous Song of Moses following the passage
of the Israelites through the Red Sea:

---

[35] Koehler, Ludwig, and Baumgartner, Walter, eds., *Lexicon in Veteris Testamenti
Libros*, E. J. Brill, Leiden, 1958.
  Books in which some form of the root of *go'el* occurs (only one citation given,
even when more than one occurs):
  Gen. 48:16 Josh. 20:3 Jer. 50:34 Ps. 19:15 Ezra 2:62
  Ex. 6:6 2 Sam. 14:11 Hos. 13:14 Prov. 23:11 Neh. 7:64
  Lev. 25:25 1 King. 16:4 Micah 4:10 Job 19:25
  Num. 35:12 Isaiah 47:4 Zeph. 3: 1 Lam. 3:58
  Deut. 19:6 Ezek. 11:15 Mal. 1: 7 Dan. 1:8
  Re land, tithe, or person in servitude: Lev. 25, 27, and Jer. 32:7f.
  Re avenger: Num. 35:12ff., Dt. 19:6f., Josh. 20:3ff., 2 Sam. 14:11
  Re defile: Isaiah 59:3, 63:3; Zeph. 3:1; Lam. 4:14; Mal. 1:7f; Ezra 2:62; Neh.
7:64, 13:29; Dan. 1:8

In Your love You led the people You *redeemed;*
In Your strength You guide them to Your holy abode.

Ex. 15:13

We find it also among the earliest prophets, as in Hosea, where God, although angered at Israel's sins, says,

From Sheol itself I will save them,
Redeem them from very death.

13:14

God is the *go'el* in Jeremiah 50:34:

Their *Redeemer* is mighty,
His name is Lord of Hosts.

And it occurs frequently in Isaiah:

For He who made you will espouse you –
His name is "Lord of Hosts."
The Holy One of Israel will *redeem* you.

54:5

And all mankind shall know
That I the Lord am your Saviour,
The Mighty One of Jacob, your *Redeemer.*

49:26

We see then that here the word *go'el* means something more than merely a near kinsman. It is in fact a divine, an archetypal image, which the word describes. It is no kinsman that Job refers to when he says:

But I know that my Redeemer (*go'el)* lives.

Job, 19:25

The kinsman, when he is designated as *go'el,* is much more the human carrier of an archetypal function. Thus, when Boaz is referred to simply as a kinsman, he is called *moda* (as in 2:1: "And Naomi had a kinsman ..." and in 3:2: "Now there is our kinsman Boaz"), or he is "of the family of Elimelech" (as in 2:1

and 2:3) or he is a *karov* (as in 2:20: "the man is related to us.").

This last sentence in itself shows that *go'el* means more than merely "kinsman." What Naomi says in 2:20 is "The man is related (*karov*) to us, he is one of our *go'alim* (=plural of *go'el)* redeeming kinsmen." With the use of the word *go'el* here, it is not the kinship but the redemptive function of the kinsman which is in the foreground.

We need to know these meanings and the various connotations of the word *go'el* in order to see the full or deeper meaning of the story of Ruth. Where the verb, *ga'al* refers to a human being, and only there, the traditional English translations render it "to do the part of a kinsman." Where it concerns a parcel of land, as in chapter four, they show no such qualms in translating it as "redeem." A reluctance to ascribe so divine a prerogative as redemption of a soul, to a human being, may well be one of the reasons why the translators refrain from using the verb "redeem" in these instances. But the word eminently fits, and is a further indication of the archetypal, or mythological, nature of our story.

When Naomi learns of the name of Ruth's benefactor, she recognizes his kinship, and tells Ruth he is their *go'el.*

> Ruth the Moabite said, "He even told me, 'Stay close by my workers until all my harvest is finished.'" And Naomi answered her daughter-in-law Ruth, "It is best, daughter, that you go out with his girls, and not be annoyed in some other field." (2:21f)

It is likely that Naomi, a wise old woman, already has an eye toward an ultimate marriage between Boaz and Ruth, a union which would constitute a restoration of their reduced estate. The mother guides the daughter along the path toward fulfillment. This will be seen more clearly in the next chapter. Ruth heeded Naomi's advice.

So she stayed close to the maidservants of Boaz, and gleaned until the barley harvest and the wheat harvest were finished. Then she stayed at home with her mother-in-law. (2:23)

Chapter Three

1. The Relationship between Naomi and Ruth

We saw in chapter two how Ruth, taking the initiative in seeking sustenance for her mother-in-law and herself, found it in the field of Boaz, whose marked attention she evoked. Naomi informed her that he was their *go'el*, and bid her to continue gleaning there. She did so, staying close to his maidens, and dwelling with Naomi throughout the harvest. In other words, even though it was in the domain of the masculine that Ruth gathered her nourishment, she stayed close to the feminine side.

Her devotion to the older woman proved to be not just a one-sided relationship, for now Naomi takes the lead in guiding Ruth. This has its parallel in personal psychology, for caring for and submitting to the Self-figure, the inner central authority in the unconscious (not to be confused with the "super-ego"), also produces the effect of being guided toward one's self-realization, and there too, sometimes via apparently unorthodox means. In our story, Naomi, seeking Ruth's fulfillment, lays out a plan of action well calculated to bring about her aim. Startlingly enough, it sounds like pure seduction.

> Naomi, her mother-in-law, said to her, "Daughter, I must seek a home for you, where you may be happy. Now there is our kinsman Boaz, whose girls you were close to. He will be winnow-

ing barley on the threshing floor tonight. So wash yourself, anoint yourself, dress up, and go down to the threshing floor. But do not disclose yourself to the man until he has finished eating and drinking. When he lies down, note the place where he lies down, and go over and uncover his feet and lie down. He will tell you what you are to do." (3:1-4)

The decision about "what you are to do" is left to Boaz, but this is a thoroughly feminine way of provoking a man into action. In fairness to Naomi it must be said that Boaz, being the *go'el,* was obligated to marry Ruth. That this, like levirate marriage, was one of the duties of the *go'el,* is shown by Boaz's acceptance of such obligation (3:12f.). He had already shown a good deal of interest in her, and one might have expected him to act on his apparent feelings. He had had ample time to do this. Ruth had been gleaning on his field from the beginning of the barley harvest until the end of the wheat harvest, a period of some seven weeks (Schauss, p. 41). Having failed to respond to his duty or his feelings, Naomi chose "a woman's way" to make him aware of them. Making a man aware of his feelings is a typical feminine function. It acts from within in a man who has a good connection with his eros or feeling side, but if he is cut off from eros, it acts from without, in the guise of a woman (cf. Jung, "The Relations between the Ego and the Unconscious," CW 7, par. 296), as is the case in our story.

Having assumed earlier that Ruth represents that feminine, eros, component which the Hebrews earlier had perforce pushed aside, as described above (p. 16f.), we might expect this move to be initiated by her. But all femininity had not been lost to the Israelites. Naomi represents the femininity in our original family quaternity. Her acceptance of the Moabitess Ruth, Ruth's cleaving to her, identifying with her, restored to Naomi a fuller femininity. Naomi is, after all, the older, the wiser, the mother figure, now enriched by Ruth, and lately being nourished by her. Further, if we read the text exactly as it is *written,* (the Masoretic *Ketiv* – as distinct from the *Qere* –

the way it was to be read, according to an ancient oral tradition "handed down to Moses at Sinai," [per R. Isaac, in the 3rd Cent. C. E.] and added to in succeeding centuries, to insure against textual changes in copying), we find in this passage a curious "slip of pen" which occurs twice, and which, interpreted psychologically, hints at an identification with Ruth on the part of Naomi. Translating the text literally, Naomi tells Ruth to wash, anoint and dress herself, "and *I* will go down to the threshing floor," and later she tells Ruth to "go over and uncover his feet and *I* will lie down."

Joüon, Sasson, and other scholars inform us that the spelling in these two instances is that of an older form of spelling for the second person singular. Still, it is strange that out of eight verbs in the imperative in this passage, just these two should have retained a spelling, which, at the time of writing was already in use for the first person. The Midrash Ruth R. (p. 70), taking note of the *Ketiv* explains it to signify that "my merits will descend with you" (to the threshing floor), which comes closer to the point, hinting at the inner union between these two representatives of the feminine principle. It is nevertheless striking that there should be two such "slips of pen" at just this point.

Many, if not most of the commentators, go to great lengths to "explain away" the clear intent of Naomi's advice, to "purify" it into a mere act of piety towards the dead. The assurances she had of Ruth's firm chastity and of Boaz's religious gravity "made her think that design safe which to others would have been perilous." (Slotki, p. 57). Ruth is merely presenting a symbolic request for the marriage which is her right (Haller, p. 13). Ruth's purity and virtue are beyond suspicion. "She is fulfilling a duty of love and piety towards the dead by approaching Boaz and reminding him of his obligation as kinsman" (Nowack, cited by Slotki, p. 57). Putting herself into so embarrassing a situation is a heroic act of loyalty. She is not seeking anything for herself, but only an heir for her husband. (Gunkel, "Ruth," p. 59). She is lauded as a properly submissive and obedient daughter (Joüon, p. 70, Rudolph, p. 32,) etc.

All these apologia are not really necessary, and only becloud the symbolic meaning of the story. With the observation that Ruth is submissive to Naomi, there can be no objection.

> She replied, "I will do everything you tell me." She went down to the threshing floor and did just as her mother-in-law had instructed her. Boaz ate and drank, and in a cheerful mood went to lie down beside the grain pile. Then she went over stealthily and uncovered his feet and lay down. In the middle of the night, the man gave a start and pulled back – there was a woman lying at his feet! (3:5-8)

Still, it is legitimate to ask why Naomi used such a suspect method to put Ruth's claim to Boaz. Was she merely utilizing a harvest celebration to bring about a match, lacking a better way? So thinks Robertson, observing that in those days women lacked power and importance, "but Naomi, like Tamar, knew of a power which can bend man to woman's will – the power of sexual attraction." (p. 213). Possibly, but such a crude calculating attitude doesn't fit well with Naomi's delineation in the rest of the story. For a better understanding of this episode it is necessary to look into some ancient religious practices, and also into the nature of the threshing floor and the role it played in them.

2. The Role of the Threshing Floor

The Israelites, in their conquest of Canaan, took over many of the local customs and also the local holy places (Goff, p. 152). As the Bible scholar and historical writer Dr. Elias Auerbach pointed out in a lecture at the University of Zurich (Nov. 8, 1954), "The religions change, but the holy places remain." As, for instance, Mount Moriah in Jerusalem, the site of the Temple. Before the construction of the Temple this was a holy site for the Jebusites, and since the destruction of the second Temple (70 C. E.) there followed on the same site a Roman temple, various Christian churches, and the still present Mosque of Omar.

In ancient agricultural societies, as was the case in Canaan, where the god and/or goddess of grain played a leading role, the threshing floor itself was often a holy place (May, pp. 75ff). The very Temple on Mount Moriah in Jerusalem was built on what had been a threshing floor (2 Chron. 3:1) where the angel of the Lord had appeared to David, on which occasion the prophet Gad

> came to David the same day and said to him, "Go and set up an altar to the Lord on the threshing floor of Arauna the Jebusite."
>
> 2 Sam. 24:18

The threshing floor would be the natural scene of revelry in celebrating the harvest festivals, and not only among the pagans. We read "Boaz ate and drank, and in a cheerful mood went to lie down beside the grain pile." In the ordinances concerning harvest festivals, the Bible specifically directs that

> You shall rejoice before the Lord your God with your son and daughter, your man-servant and your maid-servant, the Levite in your communities, and the stranger, the fatherless, and the widow in your midst ...
>
> Deut. 16:11, modified

and repeats these injunctions in verses 14 and 15: "You shall rejoice in your festival ..." and "... you shall have nothing but joy."

Harvest festivals among the pagans were often a licentious orgy in which sexual promiscuity was of the nature of a religious rite (Gaster, pp. 24ff). There is no doubt that the Hebrews took over such practices from their neighbors, as we can see from the condemnations of the prophets against their adoption of the heathen orgies. For example in Hosea 9:1:

> Rejoice not, O Israel,
> As other peoples exult;
> For you have strayed
> Away (literally, gone a-whoring) from your God:
> You have loved a harlot's fee
> By every threshing floor of new grain.

It is not unlikely that this verse, as May surmises (p. 76), has reference to hierodules, "sacred prostitutes." The Hebrew term for hierodule is *kedeshah* (related to the word *kadosh*, "holy," "set apart"), whereas the term for prostitute per se, is *zonah*. Both terms, unfortunately, are rendered alike, "harlot," in many English translations. (Not, naturally, in scholarly commentaries. The New JPS translation "into the language of contemporary English speakers" used here for the most part, renders it as "cult prostitute" on two occasions (Gen. 38:21 and Dt. 23:18), but also as "prostitute" alone elsewhere. Hierodulism was not, of course, an official part of the Hebrew religion. Nevertheless, the Bible frequently states that the people sinfully observed these heathen practices (1 Kings 14:24; 15:12; 22:47; 2 Kings 23:7; Hos. 4:14). During the reign of Rehoboam, son of Solomon, we read:

> And there were also male cult prostitutes in the land. They did according to all the abominations of the nations which the Lord drove out before the people of Israel.
>
> 1 Kings 14:24, R. S. V.

There were also male hieroduloi, *kadesh* in Hebrew, rendered male cult prostitutes in the Revised Standard Version cited here, (the New JPS translation omits the word "cult" on occasion), and which other translations give as "sodomites." In the plural, the term is used collectively and of both sexes (I. W. Slotki, Kings, SBB, p. 108). Hierodules even penetrated into the Temple, whence they were banished by the reforms instituted by King Josiah (2 Kings 23:7) in the 7th century, B. C. E.

And he broke down the houses of the cult prostitutes
(pl. *kedeshim*)
which were in the house of the Lord. (R. S. V.)

When Hosea says "You have loved a harlot's fee by every threshing floor of grain," he uses neither the word *kedeshah* nor *zonah*, but a word *etnan*, "a harlots fee" (from a root meaning "give," "distribute gifts"), which is applied to both "profane" and "sacred" prostitutes. But in an earlier chapter (4:14) he links the two. In a condemnation of the pagan practices of Israel, described as harlotry, he says

> For they themselves turn aside with whores (literally, *zonoth*, prostitutes)
> And sacrifice with prostitutes (literally, *kedeshoth*, hierodules)

This verse, according to the famous Jewish commentator of the middle ages, David Kimchi (1160-1235), refers to association with temple harlots. (S. M. Lehrman, in The Twelve Prophets, SBB, p. 17)

We also find the word *etnan* applied to *kedeshoth* in the law prohibiting them, Deut. 23:18f.

> No Israelite woman shall be a cult prostitute (*kedeshah*) nor shall any Israelite man be a cult prostitute (*kadesh*). You shall not bring the fee of a whore (*etnan zonah*) or the pay of a dog into the house of the Lord your God.

Here we see the word *etnan*, and even the word *zonah*, associated with hierodules. The curious phrase, "pay of a dog," which stands parallel to "fee of a whore," apparently refers to the male *kadesh*. This becomes more understandable in the light of evidence (E. R. E. vi, p. 674b; Riehm, ii, p. 1727) that at the temple at Kition in Cyprus, there were male hieroduloi who were referred to as "dogs," and that *kinaidoi*, "dogs," was the general Greek term for the eunuch priests of the Mother Goddess. The very presence of the Deuteronomic law indicates the existence of a practice against which it was necessary to legislate.

It is permissible to assume from Hosea's reproach that rites involving *kedeshoth*, hierodules, took place on the threshing floors, and this, presumably, would be during the harvest festivals. Such were common practices in the ancient world. We find the institution of hierodulism in Babylon, Syria, Egypt, Cyprus, etc. The functions of the hierodule or *kedeshah* were not limited to the holidays. She played a significant role at the harvest festivals where the *hieros gamos,* the sacred marriage, was a central feature (Gaster, pp. 24f, 232ff). The hierodule was, after all, a priestess or representative of the goddess. The great mother goddess, under whatever name she was worshipped, Ishtar, Isis, Astarte, Aphrodite, was associated with a lover, Tammuz, Osiris, Adonis, with whom she mated year by year. This union of the divine pair, the *hieros gamos,* was enacted by the priest or priestess on earth (Frazer, p. 299).

3. The Hierodule and Daughter Aspects of Ruth

It was at a yearly harvest festival that Adonis was begotten through the incestuous union of King Kinyras with his daughter Myrrh (Frazer, p. 300). We already pointed out the similarity between this story and that of Lot and his daughters. There is still another Biblical story of father-daughter incest which is in close relationship to the story of Ruth; that of Tamar and Judah (see above, p. 50).

Like Ruth, Tamar was a childless widow – like Ruth, she was entitled to a levirate marriage – and like Ruth, she achieved her aim by "seducing" her kinsman, her father-in-law, Judah. Boaz, though not her father-in-law, was appreciably older than Ruth in the feeling of the story, and gives the impression of a "father-figure." He refers to Ruth as "my daughter" (2:8, 3:11) and legend makes him the brother of Elimelech. Also, according to legend, he was 80 years old, and Ruth, 40 (Ginzberg, vi, 188; Ruth R. 75f).

The similarity between Ruth and Tamar is alluded to in the story itself when the people say to Boaz, "... let thy house be like the house of Perez, whom Tamar bore unto Judah...." (4:12). According to a Kabbalistic legend Ruth is, in fact, the re-incarnation of Tamar (Müller, p. 136). And the Bible refers to Tamar as a *kedeshah*.

> He (Judah's messenger) inquired of the people of that town, "where is the cult prostitute (*kedeshah*), the one at Enaim...."
>
> Gen. 38:21

Judah had not recognized her because

> ... she took off her widow's garb, covered her face with a veil, and, wrapping herself up, sat down at the entrance to Enaim.... When Judah saw her, he took her for a harlot (*zonah*); for she had covered her face.
>
> Gen. 38:14f

The veil was a sign of Ishtar, belonged to the cult of the goddess, and was worn by the *kadishtu*, (the Akkadian term corresponding to the Hebrew *kedeshah*) who was dedicated to her (R. Kluger, 1991, p. 32ff). Jeremias (p. 381) assumes that Ruth veiled herself, in his understanding of Naomi's instruction to "put thy raimant upon thee" (older JPS translation, more literal than 'dress up') when she went to the threshing floor. Judah had offered Tamar a kid from the goats of his flock, and Gunkel remarks (p. 416) that this was the customary gift to the hierodule, since the goat was holy to the love goddess, and was her sacrificial animal. He points out another echo of the myth of Ishtar, whose love was fatal, in the death of the two husbands of Tamar. Judah, in fact, withheld his third son "– for he thought, 'He too might die like his brothers.'" (Gen. 38:11). This theme is repeated in a weaker form in "Ruth" in the early death of Mahlon.

We see a similar "weakening" of the incest motif in these three Biblical stories. In the oldest (J text) story, Lot's daughters commit incest with their natural father. In the next

(E text) story, the incest is between Tamar and her father-in-law. In the latest story it is between Ruth and a "father-figure" (see below, p. 93).

Ishtar's lover Tammuz was a god, and he could be brought back to life. On this occasion the *kadishtu* also played a role, "putting his mind at ease," as we read in the myth "Ishtar's Descent to the Underworld" (Heidel, p. 127). After Ishtar's return to the upper regions, Ereshkigal, the queen of the underworld, sent Tammuz back to her. It is interesting to compare the instructions given for Tammuz when he is sent to rejoin Ishtar, with those given to Ruth.

> As for Tammuz (her) youthful husband
> *Wash* him with pure water and *anoint* him with precious oil.
> *Clothe* him with a red garment and let him play upon the flute of lapis lazuli ...
> Let the courtesans (*kadishtu*) put his mind at ease.

These were the preparations for Tammuz's re-union with the Queen of Heaven, goddess of love and fertility. Naomi's instructions to Ruth to wash, anoint, and clothe herself (best clothes are apparently meant), can be understood as simply to make herself pleasing to Boaz, but sound more like a ceremonial instruction, as for a bride – or to prepare for a *hieros gamos*. So, in the passage from Ezekiel quoted earlier (p. 47) where God "spread His robe (wing) over Jerusalem (=Israel),

> ... and I entered into a covenant with you by oath – declares the Lord God; thus you became Mine. I *bathed* you in water ... and *anointed* you with oil. I *clothed* you with embroidered garments..."
>
> Ezek. 16:8-10

This was a process of purification, of sanctification (*kedeshuth*). Similarly, before the high priests could administer to God at the altar, they were required to wash and anoint themselves, and to clothe themselves in special garments (Ex. 30:21, 30; 31:10). They too, had to be sanctified.

There is no direct reference to Ruth as a *kedeshah*, but in view of the parallels with the Tamar story, and the functions of the hierodules, and of the usages on the threshing floors, and the instructions of Naomi, the occurrence in our story may be seen as something other than a mere profane seduction scene. Nevertheless, we cannot overlook the definite aura of seduction, by a young woman, of an older man, and that while he is under the influence of wine.

4. Boaz and Ruth in the Light of Mythological Parallels

A comparison with other myths shows that the motif of seduction, as well as that of incest, though perhaps not so frequently, is involved with the birth of a divine figure or hero. Understood symbolically, this may be seen as indicating that the longed-for birth of a savior is not achieved in a simple straight-forward manner.

Ruth's behavior at the threshing floor reflects in a milder form, that of her ancestors. Lot's daughters made him drunk, and from his union with the elder, sprang Moab, father of a people. So also Myrrh, who, under the influence of the love goddess Aphrodite (Gunkel, p. 218; Kerényi, p. 75) seduced her father, King Kinyras, by making him drunk, and bore Adonis, a god. Adonis, the beloved of Aphrodite, was confined to the underworld and its queen, Persephone, for part of the year, during which time nothing grew on earth. The same was the case when Tammuz, the beloved of Ishtar, was subject to queen Ereshkigal of the Babylonian underworld, for part of the year.

Persephone had become queen of the underworld after being kidnapped and seduced by its ruler Hades, brother of Zeus. Her disappearance led to the anguished search for her by her inconsolable mother Demeter, the grain goddess. Only after the mother and daughter were united, did the barley and other grains grow again. But not, and from then on, during the third of the year during which Persephone was in the netherworld. However, in the network of Greek myths we find (Kerényi, 1949, 1951) that it was Zeus himself who seduced Persephone, and that this was actually arranged by her mother, Demeter – who herself was seduced by Zeus!! Further, in the Eleusinian mysteries, which centered about the cult of Demeter and Persephone, there took place a *hieros gamos*, and the birth of a child was announced, but whether it was born to Persephone or to Demeter is not clear. This child was Dionysus, and he, like Tammuz and Adonis, was especially a woman's divinity. During one of the cult's religious processions, Dionysus, or rather the phallus representing him, was carried in a *liknon*, a winnowing fan, under a pile of fruit, and was 'awakened' by the women who served him. In our story, Boaz was winnowing at night on the threshing floor, and when he later lay down at the pile of grain, Ruth "went over stealthily and uncovered his feet and lay down."

It may be, as some maintain (May, p. 77; Robertson, p. 217) that this expression is a euphemism. In the Kabbalah Boaz is equated with a divine force expressing itself in the lower (earthly) level as sexual desire, and the name Boaz, "in him is strength," alludes to the erected phallus.[36] The Zohar, commenting on this passage in its discussion of the Tamar story (vol. ii, p. 218) says,

> "Tamar enticed Judah.... Ruth similarly enticed Boaz, as it say 'and she uncovered his feet and laid her down.'"

It says of Tamar that she committed incest, but that it was all ordained from on high: "there were two women from whom the seed of Judah was to be built up, from whom were to descend King David, King Solomon, and the Messiah, viz. Tamar and Ruth. These two women had much in common." And a little later, "... we do not ask why Obed was not born

---

[36] I am indebted to Prof. Gershom Scholem for this information.

from another woman, for assuredly Ruth was necessary for that purpose." This mystic book sees Ruth's action as seduction, if not, by analogy, as incest. Incest is viewed by Kabbalists as a holy union, hence it is forbidden to men, for it may not be profaned by earthly sensuality (Burnstein, viii, p. 468). The incestuous *hieros gamos* is a divine prerogative, out of which is born the divine child.

The union of Ruth and Boaz is not overtly incestuous, but it should be noted that both parties are descended from incestuous unions, Boaz from Judah and Tamar, and Ruth from Lot and his daughter. And from the child of their union will descend King David, and ultimately, the Messiah.

5. Some Kabbalistic Interpretations of Boaz and Ruth

Not only will this union give rise to a figure which is a representation of fulfillment, but it in itself represents a fulfillment, a completion, a redemption. We already mentioned the legend (p. 44) according to which God lost something valuable among the Moabites, namely Ruth. Her union with Boaz represents the restoration of this "lost dove." To return to our text: Boaz awoke startled to find a woman at his feet.

> "Who are you?" he asked. And she replied, "I am your handmaid Ruth.
> Spread your robe (literally, wing) over your handmaid, for you are a redeeming kinsman (*go'el*)." (3:9)

We already (p. 47) drew attention to the same metaphor, used in Ezekiel 16:8:

> ... I passed by you and saw that your time for love had arrived. So I spread my robe (wing) over you and covered your nakedness, and I entered a covenant with you by oath – declares the Lord God; thus you became Mine.

The comparison is strikingly enforced in the light of the interpretation which the Kabbalistic work "Zohar Ruth" (p. 126a) gives to our passage: Ruth, whose name is interpreted as "turtle dove" (see p. 44, above), personifies the *Knesseth Yisrael*, (Community of Israel), and also the *Shekhinah*, God's feminine side who, like Israel, is in exile. What the Zohar Ruth perceives in this scene between Boaz and Ruth, *is a representation of God, the Go'el Yisrael, the Redeemer of Israel, taking her back, i.e., God redeeming His (feminine side, the) Shekhinah.*

This interpretation by the Zohar Ruth, which was written before 1280 according to Scholem (p. 188, p. 162), is in basic agreement with the legend of the "lost value" which is probably centuries older, and both are consonant with the understanding of our story when it is viewed symbolically. The plot of the story, magnificently developed, builds up to this point of the *ge'ullah*, the redemption of this foreign yet related figure of Ruth the Moabite, with all which this implies, and its consequences. Boaz answers Ruth's request.

> He exclaimed, "Be blessed of the Lord, daughter! Your latest deed of loyalty[37] (*hesed*) is greater than the first, in that you have not turned to younger men, whether poor or rich." (3:10)

Boaz's gratitude reveals that *the masculine spirit, the Yahwistic spirit, which he exemplifies, is not only the redeemer, but itself is in need of the loyalty of the feminine side.* We find a similar need and desire expressed by God himself toward Israel personified as a woman (R. Kluger, 1950). So, for example, when God complains of Israel that

> She would go after her lovers,
> Forgetting me
> – declares the Lord.

[37] The Hebrew word *hesed* here, is elsewhere translated as "kindness," as in verses 1:8 and 2:20. Its meanings embrace "mercy," "grace," loving kindness," "loyalty," "goodness."

Assuredly,
I will speak coaxingly to her ...
And speak tenderly to her ...
... ...
And in that day
– declares the Lord –
You will call [Me] Ishi (My husband),
And no more will you call me Baali

> (My master & the Canaanite god).

... ...
And I will espouse you with faithfulness;

> Hosea, 2:15-23

It was the feminine (earth) in contrast to the masculine (spiritual) principle in Israel which "went a-whoring" (so the Hebrew) after the foreign gods (Deut. 31:16), and "committed great harlotry" by forsaking the Lord (Hosea 1:2), wherefore, as already noted, the necessity for repressing the feminine principle. In our story, Ruth, representing the repressed feminine, did not "turn to younger men," but channeled her natural instincts in the interest of her remaining with the newer masculine spirit, which proved to be a requisite for redemption. Ruth's request to be united with Boaz will, it seems, be fulfilled.

And now daughter, have no fear. I will do in your behalf whatever you ask, for all the elders of my town (lit. "gate of my people") know what a fine woman you are. (3:11)

However there is still an obstacle to the redemption.

But while it is true that I am a redeeming kinsman, there is another redeemer closer than I. Stay for the night. Then in the morning, if he will act as a redeemer, good! let him redeem. But if he does not want to act as redeemer for you, I will do so myself, as the Lord lives! Lie down until morning. (3:12, 13)

> [A number of other translations have here for the word "redeem," "do the part of a kinsman (to)"]

THE SEFIROTH

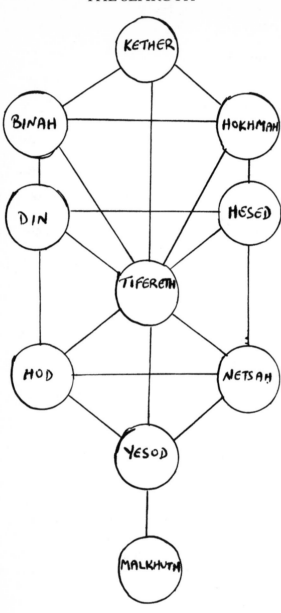

THE SEFIROTH

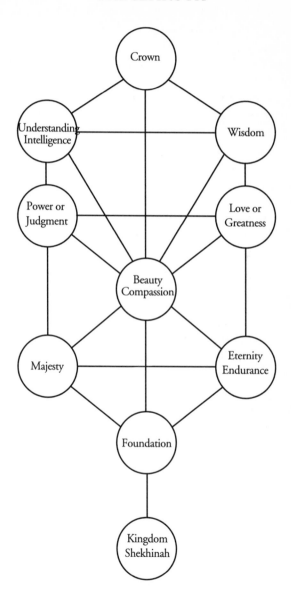

Who is this closer redeemer? He is never named. Obviously he is a relative of Boaz, and stands between him and Ruth. This anonymous, unknown figure strikes the reader as a danger, despite, or even because of, his prior right, even obligation, to the redemption. He looms as a menacing shadow to what we instinctively feel would be the right solution. In fact we can, psychologically speaking, understand him as a shadow figure of Boaz, with whom he has to come to terms before he can redeem Ruth. (The shadow is the term for those, usually negative, qualities of the individual of which he is not conscious, or which he denies, which are generally projected onto others – like the pot calling the kettle black.) We will discuss this aspect of the nearer *go'el* when we meet him in the next chapter.

Most interesting and pertinent for the symbolic under-standing of our material, are some remarks of the mystical book Zohar Ruth (p. 127a) on this passage about the "closer" and the "farther" *go'alim*. They are identified as the two Messiahs, the Messiah ben David, and his forerunner, the Messiah ben Joseph. Without going into the intricacies of this interpretation, suffice it for us to note that *go'el*, redeemer, is understood in its higher, Messianic sense.

Further, the two *go'alim* are equated with two of the ten *Sefiroth* – the Kabbalistic conception of "the ten emanations of divine manifestation in which God emerges from his hidden abode ...," the emanations, aspects, or attributes of the Godhead. "He is they, and they are He.... The world of the Sefiroth is described as a mystical organism.... The two most important images used in this connection are that of the tree – see the drawing – and that of the man." (Scholem, p. 213f) In the latter, the various *Sefiroth* are related to the parts of the body, and the ninth *Sefirah*, *Yesod*, 'the foundation' is corre-lated with the male sex organ.

A major contribution of the Zohar is the highly developed conception of the Shekhinah as the feminine element in God (Scholem, p. 229). "The mystery of sex, as it appears to the

Kabbalist, has a terribly deep significance. This mystery of human existence is for him ... a symbol of the love between the divine 'I' and the divine 'You,' the Holy One, blessed be He, and His Shekhinah. The *hieros gamos*, the 'sacred union' of the King and the Queen ... is the central fact.... In God there is a union of the active and the passive, procreation and conception, from which all mundane life and bliss are derived." (p. 227)

Yesod = "the 'basis' or 'foundation' of all active forces in God" stands immediately above, and is the *Sefirah* in contact with, the tenth and lowermost *Sefirah*, *Malkhuth*, "the 'kingdom' of God, usually described in the Zohar as the *Keneseth Israel*, the mystical archetype of Israel's community, or as the *Shekhinah*" (p. 213). It will be recalled that the Zohar Ruth identified Ruth with the *Shekhinah*, and identified Boaz with *Yesod*.

About *Yesod* Scholem tells us: "The ninth *Sefirah*, *Yesod*, out of which all the higher *Sefiroth* – welded together in the image of the King – flow into the *Shekhinah*, is interpreted as the procreative life force dynamically active in the universe. Out of the hidden depth of this *Sefirah* the divine life overflows in the act of mystical procreation" (i.e., a mystical *hieros gamos*). (p. 227) And later, "... the *Shekhinah* ... the last of the *Sefiroth* ... must wander into far lands ... The union of God and the *Shekhinah* constitutes the true unity of God, which lies beyond the diversity of His various aspects, *Yihud*, as the Kabbalists call it." (p. 230)

Speaking of "the exile of the *Shekhinah*" he says: "Only after the restoration of the original harmony or redemption, when everything shall occupy the place it originally had in the divine scheme of things, will 'God be One and His Name One,' in Biblical terms, truly and for all time." (p. 232)

It must be remembered that the foregoing remarks on the nature of the *Sefiroth* refer to the Zohar, which was not written with an eye to the Book of Ruth. All the more impressive is it that the Book of Ruth was found to symbolize some of these conceptions, as is brought out in the Zohar Ruth (which is an earlier one of the many writings making up the Zohar). In view of what we have learned about the *Sefiroth*, we see that the Zohar Ruth too, finds the symbolic meaning of the marriage of Ruth and Boaz to be a redemption of an "exiled" feminine aspect, a restoration of harmony and unity, i.e., of wholeness.

6. Boaz's Acceptance

But the redemption does not yet take place. Boaz sends Ruth away while it is still dark.

> So she lay at his feet until dawn. She rose before one person could distinguish another, for he thought, "Let it not be known that the woman came to the threshing floor." (3:14)

This apparently is a matter of guarding their reputation, and also a precaution, as Rowley notes (p. 181), against any claims by the nearer *go'el* that his rights had been prejudiced. Symbolically however, it shows that this occurrence must be kept from public knowledge. As we saw in verse 8, it happened "in the middle of the night," that magical momentous time, and he sends her away before it is light; i.e., this meeting took place in the dark, in the unconscious, so to speak. That is where Boaz was faced with his obligations, and where he became, or was made, aware of his feelings. Such may often be the case with anyone; dreams can bring to our attention situations and feelings of which we are not consciously suffi-ciently aware. Boaz does not reject or dismiss Ruth. It is an effective meeting. He accepts her. He even gives her a gift for Naomi, which is in effect an indication of this acceptance. But before the union can be made public – brought into full realization – a confrontation with the other *go'el* must take place. Besides, traditional forms must be respected. The consent of the whole community is required to make the union valid. In modern psychological terms we would say that the conscious and the unconscious must be in harmony for there to be any such thing as "redemption," being whole. Boaz acts to implement his feeling

> And he said, "Hold out the shawl you are wearing." She held it while he measured out six measures of barley, and he put it on her back. (3:15)

This gift is for Naomi, as we learn later, and in view of the conditions under which it is given, it is obviously an acknowledgment of the purpose of Ruth's visit, and hence may be construed as a betrothal gift for her mother-in-law. In the text, the measure is not stated. The Hebrew reads "six barley (grains)." It is generally accepted, in agreement with the Targum (an early Aramaic translation) that six *seahs* are meant, which would be some 42 kilograms according to Rudolph, or 72 liters according to Joüon. This would be a rich gift, perhaps the most a woman could carry on her head or her shoulder. (Our translation has it that Boaz "put it on her back," but the Hebrew text doesn't specify where, just that he put it "on her.") The Targum adds here that Ruth received miraculous strength for the occasion (Hartmann, p. 72). The Midrash Ruth R. (p. 83) sees in the number six an allusion to the six righteous men who will descend from Ruth, from David to the Messiah. From the view of number symbolism, six can be seen as symbolizing the union of masculine and feminine (3x2), as also in the union of the masculine and feminine triangles which form the six pointed star. In that the gift is for Ruth's mother-in-law, some (Staples, p. 155; May p. 77) see it as reflecting the offering to the goddess, given to the *kedeshah* who serves her. That for Naomi this gift was a sign that Boaz accepted his obligation, is clear from her reaction to it.

Ruth returns home.

> When she[38] got back to town she came to her mother-in-law, who asked, "How is it with you daughter?" She told her all that

the man had done for her; and she added, "He gave me these six measures of barley, saying to me, 'Do not go back to your mother-in-law empty-handed.'" (3:16-17)

There are those (Robertson, p. 216; May, p. 77) who believe that the text was "cleaned up" and that originally the story told of the consummation of the marriage that night. It strikes me that this is reading parallel mythological motifs literally into the story, rather than seeing the story as a different solution to an older common motif. In the absence of any manifest corruption of the text, we must accept it as it is, and try to understand what it tells us. It is true that on this point the story is rather ambiguous, yet the greater implication seems to be that Boaz did not take Ruth that night. What counts is that he fully accepted her claim ("have no fear, I will do … whatever you ask") and while noting the existence of an obstacle ("But … there is a *go'el* closer than I") pledged himself to deal with it ("as the Lord lives"), and committed himself thereto to Naomi ("Do not go back to your mother-in-law empty-handed"). The bid for the union was made in secret ("do not disclose yourself."… "she went over stealthily"), in the dark ("in the middle of the night"), i.e., in the unconscious. The legitimacy of the claim, as we have just seen, was immediately accepted, its fulfillment however, must be conscious ("in the morning"), after dealing openly with the obstacle, the nearer *go'el,* ("Boaz had gone to the gate" = the 'court of law' in those days), in the presence of the collective consciousness and knowledge ("the elders of the town").

This is the new development of the old motif of the *hieros gamos,* that it be dealt with also in consciousness, and that the unity, the wholeness, which it represents, be made real in *this* world.

Boaz sets out. Ruth's visit to him that night was the stimulus. Naomi, a sort of higher, Self figure, directing Ruth,

---

[38] so many Heb. mss.; most mss. read "he."

is now also acknowledged by Boaz, through his gift to her. Having stirred the masculine, Boaz, to activity, Naomi, the "wise old woman," gives Ruth some feminine advice.

> And Naomi said, "Sit still, my daughter, till you learn how the matter turns out. For the man will not rest, but will settle the matter today." (3:18)

Chapter Four

1. The Confrontation at the Gate

Boaz wastes no time in dealing with the problem. We read:

Meanwhile, Boaz had gone to the gate and sat down there. And now the redeemer whom Boaz had mentioned passed by. He called, "Come over and sit down here, So-and-so!" And he came over and sat down. Then (Boaz) took ten elders of the town and said, "Be seated here"; and they sat down. (4:1, 2)

The gate, in Biblical times, as throughout the ancient world, was the public place of meeting, the market place, and also the court of law. In Amos 5:15 we find: "Hate evil, love good, and establish justice in the gate." The gate corresponds to the Roman forum. It represents public knowledge, public opinion. We saw this in Boaz's remark to Ruth (3:11) "... all the elders of my town (lit. all the gate of my people) know what a fine woman you are." Psychologically seen, the gate here stands for conscious awareness and judgment.

Here it is that Boaz sits himself down, whereupon the other redeemer appears. We referred to this *go'el* as a kind of shadow figure. This is supported by the nature of Boaz's address, "So-and-so!" The Hebrew *ploni almoni*, is a phrase used to refer to some one or something that cannot or will not be named, something like the German N. N., from the Latin *nescio nomen*, name unknown. David, referring to a purportedly secret mission, uses these words to say that the men were sent

to "such and such a place"(1 Sam. 21:3). An old Latin text, the
£ text (Rudolph, p. 35) translates our passage *et ille dixit quid
secreti.* The Septuagint renders Boaz's words as "You, hidden
one," (Joüon, "o caché"; Rudolph, "Du Verborgener"), as is
also the case in an old Arabic translation which could not,
according to Joüon, have been influenced by the Septuagint.
The Targum has here "one whose ways are unknown or
hidden" (Hartmann, p. 76). Per Rudolph, a possible derivation of the Hebrew is from a root meaning "suppressed one,"
"secret one."

It is this "other one" whom Boaz calls to sit with him before
the elders of the town, at the gate. Ten men is the quorum
required by Jewish law for public prayer. Legend has it that
when ten men worship together the spirit of God Himself
comes to join them. The fact that Boaz gathers ten elders
shows that the proceedings are especially significant. Gilgamesh, although king of Uruk, felt it necessary to consult the
elders before setting out on his hazardous journey, which
meeting, incidentally, also took place at the gate, and he calls
them his counselors (Heidel, p. 37f). The term "elders of the
town" refers more to their position as leaders, magistrates,
judges, than to their age. So, for instance, the Persian magistrates were called *Acsacal,* "graybeard," regardless of their age
(Gesenius, p. 265). The position of the elders as judges can be
seen in Deut. 22: 18f: "The elders ... shall fine him a hundred
[shekels of] silver...." In our passage we see the elders as a
court; psychologically, a court of consciousness and con-
science. They represent the whole people, and by being
witnesses, they are also involved in and responsible for the
outcome.

On a personal level this may be compared, psychologically,
to an individual dealing with a "shadow problem" in full
consciousness, confronting his own darker motives, and taking the responsibility for it. This is not so easy to achieve, for
one's shadow is not always obliging enough to appear so
conveniently to ones consciousness. But if one seriously

accepts and submits to a higher inner demand, it is more likely to occur. This we may also infer from several Midrashic comments on this passage, according to which, because of Boaz's zeal in dealing with the matter, God sent an angel to lead the nearer *go'el* to the gate.

2. The Nature of the Shadow

Just what is the nature of this shadow figure which we have postulated the nearer *go'el* to be? Let us consider the dealings between him and Boaz.

> He said to the redeemer, "Naomi, now returned from the country of Moab, must sell the piece of land which belonged to our kinsman Elimelech. I thought I should disclose the matter to you and say: Acquire it in the presence of those seated here and in the presence of the elders of my people. If you are willing to redeem it, redeem! But if you will not redeem, tell me that I may know. For there is no one to redeem but you, and I come after you." "I am willing to redeem it," he replied. Boaz continued, "When you acquire the property from Naomi and from Ruth the Moabite, you must also acquire the wife of the deceased, so as to perpetuate the name of the deceased upon his estate." The redeemer replied, "Then I cannot redeem it for myself, lest I impair my own estate. You take over my right of redemption, for I am unable to exercise it." (4:3-6)

Something new and unexpected has come into the picture: the question of the purchase, or redemption of the land, since one of the rights and duties of the *go'el* is to purchase a kinsman's land which is in danger of being sold out of the family. As in Jeremiah 32:8f:

> "... buy my land ... for the right of succession is yours, and you have the duty of redemption (*ge'ulah*). Buy it." So I bought the land....

Till now in the story of Ruth, it was only the *go'el's* duty of marriage that was spoken of. In fact, we are surprised to learn that Naomi had any land to sell. Naomi may or may not have known of her claim to the land. In any case she was in no position to work it, and there is no indication that she thought of it as a pawn in her plan to find a husband for Ruth. But Boaz, a wealthy landowner, was certainly aware of the land, its value, and the laws concerning its redemption or sale. He tells the nearer *go'el*, who has the prior right of purchase. This is an agricultural community, and the *go'el*, as any astute farmer would be, is quite ready to take advantage of his right and to purchase the land, and says so. It is then that Boaz confronts him with the other duty of a kinsman, and tells him that at the same time he will "also acquire (Ruth,) the wife of the deceased so as to perpetuate the name of the deceased upon his estate."

The Hebrew word *kanah*, "to buy," rendered "acquire" in our translation, does not necessarily signify purchase in the usual sense. According to Burnstein (vol. x. p. 882) its basic meaning is "to inherit," "to obtain legally." This passage implies neither that the *go'el* has to "purchase" Ruth, nor that she is automatically a part of the property. What is indicated is akin to the levirate marriage, the "possession" of the widow as wife, in order "to perpetuate the name of the deceased."

"To perpetuate the name of the deceased" means to give Ruth a son, who would then be accounted as the son and heir of Mahlon, and thus also the heir of Elimelech. As such, the land would then revert to him. Hence the words "… upon his estate." This the nearer *go'el* is unwilling to do, "lest I impair my own estate," i.e., with an eye to his own children. His inheritance would be enriched if he bought heirless land from Naomi, who could no longer bear children. But to pay for the land, *and* to marry and support a penniless Ruth plus her mother-in-law, only to lose the land later, was not very "practical," as Rowley observes (p. 177). Thus we see that although the closer *go'el* was ready to take advantage of a right that would increase his material wealth, he was not willing to undertake a duty that entailed a material loss.

From an outer point of view, Boaz moved with great skill, as Rowley points out, in maneuvering the nearer *go'el* to renounce his prior right: it was a master stroke to introduce the question of land and so to place the *go'el* in a dilemma. Boaz apparently knew human nature, therefore he was concerned that "it be not known that the woman came to the threshing floor." If the nearer *go'el* suspected that Boaz wanted to marry Ruth, he might have needed inducing to renounce his claim, and if Boaz had acceded to Ruth's request immediately, the *go'el* could claim, with justice, that his rights had been infringed. Boaz played his cards well, and proved to be a resourceful tactician in overcoming the obstacle to his marriage to Ruth, which was presented in the person of the nearer *go'el.*

From the point of view of personal psychology, the nearer *go'el* as a shadow figure represents the materialistic attitude. On the individual level, this exists in everyone, and an apparently noble idealism can well have a root in an unconscious materialistic motivation, which thus diminishes its validity – and which may later unexpectedly appear to claim its "prior right." It were better to face it at the beginning, to "give the devil his due," to bring it into the open, to the "gate," to make it conscious. Expressed psychologically, "to confront the shadow."

There is a still broader symbolical meaning to the nearer *go'el.* He is the conservative traditional element, willing to buy the land, the inheritance of Elimelech, the old 'leading principle.' What he balks at is taking Ruth, the Moabitess, with it. While he accepts the inheritance, the 'property' of the old, the traditional masculine, he is unwilling or unable to accept the estranged, now foreign, feminine (eros) addition, to raise through her a new heir for the old heritage. He represents the old ways, opposed to a new development. There is a certain similarity here to another biblical episode: insofar as Boaz "maneuvered" the nearer *go'el* to give up his prior right, we can compare him to Jacob, who, at the instigation of Rebekah, tricked Isaac, the then blind older tradition, to give him the blessing which ordinarily would have been the "prior right" of Esau. The new development called for the re-integration of the previously repressed and now strange feminine element. A Midrashic comment (Ruth R. p. 85f) of significance to this passage holds that the nearer *go'el* refused to marry Ruth because of the law (Deut. 23:4) forbidding an Ammonite or Moabite to be "admitted into the congregation of the Lord." He was ignorant of *the new law* which had already been enacted, removing the restriction from an Ammonit*ess* and Moabit*ess*. It was with this figure that Boaz had to have an *Auseinandersetzung*, a confrontation, before the path was clear to marry Ruth.

3. The Freeing of the Way

Now this was formerly done in Israel in cases of redemption or exchange:

> to validate any transaction, one man would take off his sandal and hand it to the other. Such was the practice in Israel. So when the redeemer said to Boaz, "Acquire for yourself," he drew off his sandal. (4:7, 8)

In this symbolic act the nearer *go'el* gives up his right of *ge'ullah*, redemption, in favor of Boaz. In the law concerning levirate marriage (Deut. 25:ff) the drawing off of the shoe restores to the woman her freedom from the authority of her brother-in-law when he refuses to marry her. The shoe was a widespread symbol of power in ancient times, no less today, as seen in such expressions as "to be under someone's heel."

By this ceremony the power of the shadow *go'el* is ended, and the way is now open for a new development, for the marriage of Ruth and Boaz, with the full knowledge and consent of the community.

> And Boaz said to the elders and to the rest of the people, "you are witnesses today that I am acquiring from Naomi all that belonged to Elimelech and all that belonged to Chilion and Mahlon. I am also acquiring Ruth the Moabite, the wife of Mahlon, as my wife, so as to perpetuate the name of the deceased upon his estate, that the name of the deceased may not disappear from among his kinsmen and from the gate of his home town. You are witnesses today."
> All the people at the gate and the elders answered, "We are witnesses." (4:9-11)

4. The Blessings for the Couple and Their Implications

The people not only acknowledge this union, but proffer a remarkable blessing.

> "May the Lord make the woman who is coming into your house like Rachel and Leah, both of whom built up the House of Israel!" (4:11)

This would elevate Ruth to become another "mother of Israel," building anew the house of Israel! Rachel and Leah were the wives of Jacob, who was led in his day to extract the right of succession from his father, the blinded old tradition. It should be noted here that the deceit he and his mother practiced was in furtherance of the divine will, as Rebekah learned it when "she went to inquire of the Lord." (Gen. 25:22). There is no direct inquiry of the Lord in the Book of Ruth, but the invisible hand of God is palpably felt behind all its events, from the famine which drove Elimelech to Moab, through Ruth's happening to light on the field of Boaz, to the outcome of their marriage – and even beyond that, to God's selection of her grandson David to be king of His people. The people continue:

"Prosper in Ephrathah[39] and perpetuate your name in Bethlehem! And may your house be like the house of Perez whom
Tamar bore to Judah – through the offspring which the Lord will
give you by this young woman." (4:11, 12)

This blessing, besides evoking the ancestry of Boaz (4:18-
21) – and in fact of the entire community, who were of the
tribe of Judah – highlights the parallelism between Ruth and
Tamar, which we have already discussed. There are also some
interesting connections between our story and that of the
birth of Perez, and the legends attached to it. Perez was one of
twins. At their birth, one put out a hand, and the mid-wife
bound a crimson thread around it

> to signify: This one came out first. But just then he drew back his
> hand, and out came his brother; and she said, "What a breach
> (Heb. peretz) you have made for yourself!" So he was named
> Perez. Afterward his brother came out, on whose hand was the
> crimson thread; he was named Zerah. (Gen. 38:28-30)

Perez, as we see, means "to breach," or "a breach." Nachmanides (1194-c. 1270), a famous rabbinical commentator
and a leading Kabbalist of his period, quotes a view that Zerah
("shining," "brightness"), the brother, is a reference to the sun,
while Perez alludes to the moon, in which, except when it is
full, there is a breach. This associates Perez with the feminine
heavenly body. Nachmanides also hints at an esoteric meaning
to the name, connected with the dynasty of his descendant,
David. (Freedman, p. 241). Legend too (Ginzberg, v, p. 336),
sees in the name Perez an allusion to his descendant the
Messiah, who is called "the Breaker."

> ... I will gather the remnant of Israel;
> He who opens the breach will go up before them;
> they will break through and pass the gate ...
> Their king will pass on before them, the Lord at their head.
>   (Micah, 2:12f.)

---

[39] Ephrathah is another name applied to Bethlehem. Cf.1:2, Gen. 35:16, 19, etc.

The story of Ruth and Boaz, like the story of Tamar and Judah, and also that of Lot and his daughter, all lead to and end with, the birth of a son, and in all three cases, sons who were ancestors of David, and hence, of the Messiah. We have already pointed out the similarity in motif of these stories. In all three there was a danger that the male line would die out, and the women all used questionable means to insure its continuance. So we can view the three stories as a series, leading toward a definite goal, the birth of a Messiah.

Viewed as a series, we can observe a definite development in these acts. For one thing, there is a reduction in the degree of incest: from father, to father-in-law, to father-figure. This represents a growing humanization in that incest is a prerogative of the gods. In the second place, and parallel to this, is a growth in the degree of consciousness on the masculine side. Lot was made drunk, unconscious, in his union with his daughters. Judah was conscious in that he was awake, but he was unconscious in that he was unaware of the identity of Tamar. Boaz however, was entirely conscious, and a willing and active participant in the union with Ruth. True, he was allured, but he responded consciously. In contrast, we might say that Judah was seduced, and Lot, raped. The three stories present a growing autonomy of consciousness, of the new masculine spirit, together with a mildening of the dominating power of the unconscious, of the pagan feminine nature-spirit. This is reflected in that the incest is less concretely enacted. A great change has taken place in the nature of the relationship between the feminine and the masculine. The masculine, Boaz, lured though he was by the feminine, is not an unwitting victim. He plays an active role to achieve the union which is now mutually and *consciously* desired.

5. Marriage and the Birth of a new *Go'el*

> So Boaz took Ruth; she became his wife, and he went in unto her
> and the Lord let her conceive, and she bore a son. (4:13)

This is an immediately fruitful union, and Yahweh's direct
intervention is specified. Throughout her previous marriage
Ruth had been barren. Barrenness frequently plays a role in
the Bible. We think of Sarah (Gen. 16:1), and Rachel (Gen.
25:21), and Rebekah (Gen. 30:1f). Rivkah Kluger (1978), as
remarked earlier (p. 17) has shown how barrenness was
connected with the problem which the feminine had in being
able to comply with the necessary acceptance of the spiritual
Yahweh. She writes: "At this time of the breaking of the power
of the great mother and the birth of a new consciousness,
women found themselves being pushed into the background.
They had no relationship with the new religious sphere. They
were deprived of their inner basis, of being contained in the
mother-cult." (p. 136)

And further: "What happens now in the life of these
women? As we can see from the texts, and as we would expect
really, they are, so to speak, in a spiritual limbo. There seems
only one way open: to link up, or be linked up, with the new
spiritual reality." (p. 137)

It was this necessity of accepting the Yahweh religion,
which resulted in the suppression or loss of a degree of
femininity, and it is just this femininity, as I hope to have
shown, which returns to the Bible, i.e., to Naomi, in the form
of Ruth; Ruth who cleaved to Naomi with the words "your
God shall be my God"; Ruth who finds her *go'el,* her
redeemer, in Boaz.

It is not only Ruth who finds her fulfillment. Through her,
the feminine principle as represented by Naomi, is fulfilled, is
redeemed, as we see from the text.

> And the women said to Naomi, "Blessed be the Lord, who has
> not withheld a redeemer (*go'el*) from you today! May his name be

perpetuated in Israel! He will renew your life and sustain your old age; for he is born of your daughter-in-law, who loves you and is better to you than seven sons." (4:14, 15)

It is Naomi, the feminine principle of the Hebrew totality which we met at the beginning of our story, now enriched by the addition of Ruth, who is the recipient of the value which comes with the birth of the child. That aspect, or that kind of eros which Ruth represents, when added to Naomi, has born the *go'el*, the renewer of life for her. Ruth restored the femininity necessary for a balanced whole, and so is "better than seven sons." We again have a quaternity, making up a totality, but it now consists of two feminine and two masculine parts.

It is remarkable that the infant is called the *go'el*. He is in no wise conceivable as a *go'el* in the technical sense of one able to buy back land, or avenge blood. Indeed we have already met two men who do fit this category, so Naomi was not previously without a "close kinsman." The allusion is rather to a *go'el* in the broader sense of redeemer, as is indicated by referring to him as one who will "renew her life." The text continues:

> Naomi took the child and held it to her bosom. She became its foster mother. And the women neighbors gave him a name, saying, "A son is born to Naomi!" They named him Obed; he was the father of Jesse, father of David. (4:16, 17)

So ends the actual story of the Book of Ruth, with the mention of David. Verses 18 to 22 are a genealogy from Perez to David. This then, seems to be the purpose of the book, to recount the events that lead, eventually, to the birth of David, the anointed of the Lord, the progenitor of the Messiah.

6. The Significance of Obed, and Mythological Parallels

That Naomi took the child to her bosom and became nurse or foster mother to him evidently signifies that she was spiritual mother to him. A spiritual significance to the name Obed, which means servant, is given to it by the Midrashim (Hartmann, p. 91), which understood it to mean "the Servant of God," and to connect it to the same subsequent designation of David.

> He chose David, His servant (Ps. 78:70)
> I have made a covenant with My chosen one;
> I have sworn to my servant David: (Ps. 89:4)

The personal name Obed, or Ebed (servant), was linked with that of a god among other Semitic peoples, as a sign of submission or service to that particular god. Among the Hebrews, however, another meaning was bound with the designation Ebed. It is used about those outstanding personalities through whom God directed the fate of His people. These were God's intermediaries, His real servants. We find the designation servant of the Lord applied to such figures as Abraham (Ps. 105:6, 42), Moses (Deut. 34:5), Joshua (Josh. 24:29), various prophets, and finally to the Messiah:

> ... I am going to bring My servant the Branch. (Zech. 3:8)

Although this specific significance of Obed, servant, does not occur among other peoples, it is found in combination with the name of some gods. Names like Obed-Isis, Obed-Osiris, are found in Egypt, Carthage, etc. It is also found linked to Dionysus (von Baudissin, pp. 198, 200).

These bring to mind other resemblances between figures in mythology and the characters in our story. The motifs of mother and daughter, and of marriage by arranged seduction, which belong to the Demeter-Persephone myths, are echoed in the Naomi-Ruth story. At the celebration of the mysteries at Eleusis, the hierophant announced that "The great goddess has borne a sacred child ...," but which goddess, Demeter or Persephone, is not said (Kerényi, 1949, p. 198). The child born is Iakchos, who is Dionysus – one of whose surnames is Dimeter, "the twice-mothered."

When we enter the complicated nexus of ancient mythology we can follow innumerable threads linking one figure to another, and one motif to another, in dizzying connections. Threads lead from both Demeter and Persephone to Aphrodite, and thence to Adonis, and so to Myrrha and her father, and the temple at Paphos, shrine of Aphrodite-Astarte, with its hierodules. Adonis brings us to Tammuz, and so to Ishtar, Ashtaroth, Astarte, and so back to Aphrodite. There are connections between Demeter and Isis, between Dionysus and Osiris, etc., etc.

Among the innumerable themes expressed and repeated in the various myths, we have mentioned but a few outstanding and recurrent ones which seem pertinent to our thesis. Foremost is the presence of "the Goddess" in various aspects – mother goddess, love goddess, fertility and grain goddess; in lamentation at the death of her beloved, and rejoicing at his rebirth. She is associated with barley and wheat. She is served by hierodules or *kedeshoth*. She participates in a *hieros gamos*. She is related to or gives birth to a male god.

7. The New Mythological Development in the Book of Ruth

We have shown how these mythological motifs can be glimpsed more or less clearly also in the story of Ruth. As mentioned earlier, this does not mean that they are direct parallels or derivatives of each other. On the contrary, the Book of Ruth shows a radically different development of these archetypal situations. In all the myths mentioned, the occurrences were built around a central figure of a goddess who was the great mother, or an aspect of her. The ruling principle in every case was the feminine principle, even where a masculine god, like Zeus, was the head of the pantheon.

Whether the god was Tammuz or Adonis, etc., the new-born or resurrected male god was subordinate to the goddess, and always linked to the ever-recurring vegetative cycle. Both the goddess and the god, despite the yearly re-birth or resurrection, were eternally the same. Human-kind, although affected by these events, never participated in them in the sense of modifying them.

We see reflections of these archetypal or mythological motifs in the story of Ruth. The death and rebirth of vegetation are reflected in the famine and harvest. The death and rebirth of the god hinted at in the deaths of husbands and sons in the beginning, and later, at the end, re-marriage and "rebirth" [to raise up the name of the deceased]. The newborn is referred to in terms that allude to a divine figure, "redeemer" and "renewer of life."

For all the similarities between the myths and our story, it is the differences which are of special importance. *The events are not eternally recurring, and humankind plays the central roles in them.* The archetypal nature remains, but it is in a state of continuing development. This can best be seen by viewing the Book of Ruth in its main context – in the whole Biblical development.

Yahweh, the God without mother or wife, is in the line of earlier masculine gods who struggled to free themselves from the all-powerful mother goddess. He is "a dynamic God who forces man into a process of growing consciousness" (R. Kluger, 1978, p. 135). The continuing differentiation which takes place in the beginning book of the Bible can be seen as emphasizing the development of spiritual consciousness. We see it in the series of separations leading to the establishment of God's chosen people: Abraham separated from Lot (whose daughters made him unconscious). Then Isaac was set off from Ishmael (son of Sarah's handmaid, "a wild ass of a man"

[Gen. 16:12]), and lastly, Jacob from Esau (the "hunter, man of outdoors" [Gen. 25:27]). The cut was closer, became more discriminating each time. First it was between uncle and nephew, then between half-brothers, and lastly between twins: a distillation and re-distillation of the new spirit, so to speak.

Ultimately this led to an overweight on the masculine side, the situation illustrated at the beginning of our book. Presumably this was an inevitable result of the tremendous struggle in getting free of the powerful nature-bound cyclical hold of the feminine. On a personal level, it is a struggle which each of us, with varying degrees of awareness and success, experiences over again in the process of individual development, in the struggle of wresting consciousness from the unconscious, in which state we are born. But the unconscious, the mother, cannot be viewed only as an enemy. Ego-consciousness, after a degree of differentiation from its unconscious matrix, when and if no longer a captive son-lover, if too far removed from her, must approach her again, unite with her, in order to achieve a balanced wholeness, in order, in Jungian terminology, to realize the Self. This is no less true, even today, on a collective level.

This is what we see on an archetypal, supra-personal level, taking place in the Book of Ruth. The differentiated Yahwistic spiritual culture, represented by Elimelech and his family, descended from Abraham after his parting from Lot, goes back to the realm of Lot, stamped as it is with the nature of the feminine. But it is deadly to remain there; the men die. That is a regression, mythically expressed, to the world of the great mother goddess, "a palace which crushes the heroes within it." The nature-connected feminine element must come from there, the eros aspect of the goddess, the spirit of moon-consciousness whose softer light mildens the sharpness of differentiation by masculine sun-consciousness, and our story shows this happening. The union, or the re-union, of the feminine and the masculine, taking place in the realm of and at this stage of, masculine spirituality, results in the birth of a *go'el,* a redeemer.

This explains how it is that interpolated parts of the text came to be attached. It is generally accepted that the last verses, from 17b through 22, giving David's genealogy, are not a part of the original story. But the inner relatedness is clear, for David is the progenitor of the Messiah, and who is this child of the union of Ruth and Boaz, of the feminine and masculine principles, if not the *go'el,* the Redeemer, the universal hope for fullness and totality which is the goal of humanity's striving.

Standing in the Sandals of

NAOMI

by Nomi Kluger-Nash

Inceptions

"I love it. Even more than when I read your first version 40 years ago. It is not only rich in its interpretation but has me feeling as though I were reading a detective story, eagerly awaiting each new turn. But – for a book on the return of The Feminine, it has a decidedly masculine melody." This immediate response to my father's request for a critique was met with a sarcastic, "All right then, you write it." We threw the ball back and forth for a couple of years of mutual grumbles which happily became cooperative editing. It was suggested that I write a "companion piece" from a modern woman's subjective reactions.

Because I am a grateful student of my father's view, I have no need to write a different interpretation on the Book of Ruth. I am not sure if what I've written should be read as an additional *midrash* as much as it is to be viewed as a "jumping off place," diving into a pool of associations where some might be hard pressed to find the immediate relevance to our story. Swimming as I did into grottos and underwater caves my efforts for tight organization dissolved. While enjoying my free-float I saw the radiance of "Ruth" glimmering in light and shadow upon a multitude of experiences. Though I cannot live up to the comparison, I would still dare to say that this associative method is what both *midrashim* and Kabbalah do with the Bible. There is a definite point around which these associations cluster whose central meaning does not deviate from my father's text. I neither argue nor rearrange his insights and ideas, but I since do refer to them (as "our text") I shall expect the reader to be carrying along his interpretation as our background, while reading what I've written solely as a conversational addendum, an open letter to friends.

One Woman's Rambling View

The following then is a foray into one woman's associations to the story of a singular woman who lived through her times of birth, loss, and new life without the benefit of knowing she was one of those chosen for a story of redemption. This short story, enticing the imagination for three millennia[1], is composed of characters each of whom has an individual life and meaning. Nonetheless, each one may be read as a discrete quality within the unfolding of one complex totality, the totality of psyche. Our text does just this in interpreting the story as a momentous happening within the process of individuation of an entire people in a specific space and time. Interestingly, this is akin to an idea of Kabbalah in the *Zohar Ruth*[2] where the characters also form the totality of Soul, not however as set upon the stage of history but rather within the realm of death and transformation in the soul's journey toward its ultimate redemption.[3]

---

[1] The Book of Ruth was probably written in the 10th century B.C.E. though it refers to an earlier time – and may in fact be from an earlier story.

[2] The Zohar Ruth, in the *Midrash haNe'elam,* is now generally accepted (not totally) as being written in the 13th century by Moses de Leon in Spain.

[3] I am thinking of the psychological concept of individuation as analogous to the religious concept of redemption – and of "psyche" in its literal translation as "soul." In kabbalistic thinking redemption proceeds as a dialectical process between humanity and God, with humanity's willed actions effecting God and redounding thereby to all creation; similar in idea to Jung's dialectic between ego and Self.

Because I see no contradiction in viewing these characters as both archetypal and personally particular – as both universal themes and material instances – I will be including those images which have sprung to mind from Kabbalah, individuals' dreams and experiences as well as my own dreams and associations, such as my relationship with "The Other" in the guise of my enemy, Arab women I've known and loved. Implicit in our text's interpretation is the identity of Nature and Feminine, therefore I shall speak of the "return to nature" as echoed in the ideals of the early Zionist movements of the 1880's – experienced in the kibbutz where I was born. These associations I try to apply to our current reverberations with the feminine triad of the widow(s) Naomi-Ruth-Orpah.

Since I write this essay from my own subjectivity my examples lean on the side of feminine experience. For this I am sorry for it would be far richer, for me as well, to include both sexes. Time and space are my dictates here, so I allow myself to relax with the *vérité*, "What's good for the goose is good for the gander." I do not forget, and hope I do not let the reader forget, that the meaning in the Book of Ruth is the interplay between masculine and feminine forming a redeeming totality, inclusive of all.

Throughout these rambles I have remained struck by the story's most personal and human touch. It is just because the story is eternal that I want to tell of current associations. It is just because Naomi is such a personal figure that I want to say something personal about her.

In my musings I allow my associations comfortable leeway. Not being terribly different from other people, I let the images conjure up what they may for I believe this situation and these women are among us today – and calling for our attention.

For Abba

" 'Remember and Observe' contain the entire Torah.
'Remember' refers to the passage on the mezuzuah.
And if you should say that 'mezuzah' is a word of feminine
gender, this is indeed true; but in this passage the masculine
Is included in the feminine." [4]

Zohar Ruth

CHAPTER 1

Remembering

As a little girl I had no doubt that Naomi was a close relative of a distant past. After all, didn't we share the same name and birthplace? Even "distant past" was not the historical time of long ago but the ever-present time of a child's mythical reality, "once-upon-a-time" being the only True time. In those days gone by I had no need of looking for the *meaning* of the story, it being sufficient in itself, nor of articulating the strong image of Naomi as some budding of a Self figure. She simply *was.* She simply *is.*

I have not stayed solely with the child's point of view, nor have I thrown it out. The story I once saw so vividly still vibrates with its own splendor, heedless of anyone's interpretations. For the sake of honoring that childhood immediacy I want to recollect a memory of Naomi even as I currently think on her.

---

[4] *The Mystical Study of Ruth; Midrash Ha Ne'elam of the Zohar to the Book of Ruth,* ed. Englander and Basser, Scholars Press, 1993; Section 14, Naomi, Ruth and Boaz, p. 102. This idea comes from earlier works, refer to my section on the Sabbath.

In our kitchen, between the refrigerator and the breakfast
nook, there hung a calendar sent by a Jewish mortuary to all
Jewish families, asked for or not. We didn't ask for it, but we
used it. Each month bore an illustration of a biblical story,
richly colored and wonderfully melodramatic. The one I
remember best was a scene from the Book of Ruth. As sure as
I am that the month (probably May or June to honor
Shavu'ot[5]) did not last for years, I remain convinced that the
calendar was opened to that one picture a good deal of my
childhood. I stared at it.

Here is Naomi standing in the center; tall, strong and
beautiful, wearing flowing long robes. She is in the middle of
a flat yellow field of wild grasses and grains on a sunny day.
Her arm is protectively around a young Ruth who is embracing her, almost leaning on her. Ruth's head is against Naomi's
shoulder and their faces are turned toward each other. They
appear as a gracefully mingled unit, Naomi sturdy, Ruth lithe.
The image of embrace is poignant, especially as it stands in
relation to the rest of the scene. Far to the right of the loving
unit, walking away, almost out of the frame of the picture, is
the single sad figure of Orpah. She is weeping. One hand
covers her face while the other trails out behind her, towards
the two women from whom she is departing … as if cast out.

---

[5] Shavu'ot (literally "weeks") is the holiday during which The Book of Ruth is read.
This festive holiday initially marked the end of the 7 week grain harvest. It is
celebrated 50 days after the offering of the first *omer* (sheaf of barley) which takes
place on *Pesach* (Passover) culminating with the offering of the two loaves of
bread made from the wheat harvest. Later this holiday came to include the
spiritual meaning of commemorating God's giving not only the bounty of His
earth but of His *Torah* (Teaching), given on Mt. Sinai during the exodus from
Egypt to the Promised Land. Receiving the Torah and being "chosen" thereby by
God to belong to Him and carry out his commandments, is then celebrated on
Shavu'ot as commemorating our union with God – later reflected in the union
between Boaz and Ruth, who met during the gleaning of the grains. The
Christian rendition of this holiday is Pentecost (literally "50th," or called
Whitsunday), coming the 7th Sunday after Easter and celebrating the same idea,
i.e., actively receiving and participating in God's spirit.

The flowing robes of the three women lend a liquid motion to the still landscape.

Remembering this picture reminds me of Proverbs 3:18:

"She is a tree of life to those who hold on to her."

And with this remembrance my mind leaps to the kabbalistic images of the Sh'chinah and Tiferet as the Tree of Knowledge and the Tree of Life ...[6]

The calendar picture along with the story I knew so well told me that Naomi was the central character. A woman of courage and warmth. I knew very well what she looked like, which in those days was tantamount to knowing what she *was* like. Naomi, except for her clothes, looked very much like Mother Nature – and Mother Nature, as anyone would know, was God's wife. Apparently she's not mentioned in the Bible but at the age of 6 or 7 such details didn't bother me. These women somehow belonged together; beautiful, brown-skinned and benevolent, they had a ruling majesty about them. There was one essential difference: whereas Mother Nature's expression was sublime, Naomi's eyes reflected a human life of emotions and endurance. Her brown hair was partially hidden by the soft blue linen that draped about her head, gracefully falling into the folds of blue and wine colored robes, down to her sandaled feet. Mother Nature shone more. She wore no head cover. Black braids arched in a shining crown around her head and her dark eyes sparkled. She was adorned with gold loop earrings, a white ruffled blouse and a long, velvety tiered skirt of russet. Such was my image of Godwife.

---

[6] The Sh'chinah is The Divine Presence, in feminine quality; God's "indwelling," while Tiferet (Beauty) is the masculine emanation of God, the central s'fira also representing Compassion, and is the Sh'chinah's lover, from whom "she" receives the divine abundance to pass on to the world below. ["I am not using the standard transliterations of the Hebrew words, as Part I does, but am preferring to use a spelling that conveys a closer pronunciation to the Hebrew."]

I never thought on these images. It all came very naturally and contained, clearly or dimly, all that was Known. Now I am not so wise. Knowing does not come so simply, and all that remains are the moods and the pictures of the story.

CHAPTER 2

Wondering on Naomi

Reading again The Book of Ruth the mood returned to me full blown: "This is a woman's story!" – and – "This is a story of love!" I was pleased to find out as if for the first time. Also, my childhood conception of Naomi's centrality was still with me. "Why is this not called the Book of Naomi?"

The obvious answer of why not came to me as I reasoned with myself, "After all, Ruth is the new element, the new woman who because of love broke the bonds with her past and united with Naomi. It is Ruth's womb which bears the redeeming child, the forerunner of the Messiah. Ruth *embodies* the *meaning* of the book."

Nevertheless my first and lasting impression is of Naomi as Leading Lady. If Ruth embodies the meaning then Naomi as Mother is the *ground* of that meaning. Her endurance, her ability to bear, even while barren, and to be – almost in spite of herself – the creating force. Paramount in my thoughts of her is that she alone is the one who visibly *changes*, who goes *through* anything, excepting of course that intensely moving scene, "on the way," between the three women. Here Ruth is certainly the mover as she clings to Naomi. The scene culminates in Ruth's insistent choice, that decisive moment upon which the entire drama hangs:

Walking the many weeks' trek from Moab to Bethlehem, Naomi stops and says, "Turn back my daughters." There are tearful pleadings but eventually the two sisters-in-law split, going their separate ways. Orpah back to her "mother's house," Naomi and Ruth forward to Bethlehem. With a heart wrenching parting, the sister unity of Orpah-Ruth is split apart; with declarations of intense devotion, the budding of a dual unit, Naomi-Ruth, is born. Orpah's splitting off is a sad but necessary happening, leaving a story still to be told of "Orpah-Redemption," a task which I believe is ours today.

Outside of that suspenseful scene I felt the entire story to be beautiful but one too neatly composed. Elimelech, Machlon and Chilion do no more than define the stage before they are dispensed with ... Ruth and Boaz accomplish with dramatic grace, and at the appointed times, their appropriate actions of love and devotion ... the elders at the gate are nameless in their role as the collective ... and the women of Bethlehem speak as a chorus. I believed that Naomi alone was the suffering and transforming figure while the other characters appeared more as characterizations whose being lay solely in exemplifying the historical/divine process of redemption – all of which came about *by virtue of what happened to Naomi.* Granted such exemplification is no small matter, yet there remained the feeling of pre-set, stock characterization when compared with the emotional flexibility of Naomi. I could not understand this apparent disproportion of value.

Along came a helpful vision of the Book of Ruth as a dance which moved in combinations of order and spontaneity. Moving with a wind, Naomi dances among still characters who are in tableaux, abstract and formal. By Naomi's weaving wind dance, in and out, each tableau gains its own particular liveliness of color, form and music as it comes into play with Naomi – who in turn is moved and formed by them. It was as though I were witnessing the animating soul: enlivening, inclusive and affecting each stock propensity, as she herself comes into being.

This image of the dance allowed me to view all characters as equally valid; their full meaning lying in the interplay.

Though I still see Naomi as the (manifest) animating force, my criticism of "too neat" gave way to admiration for the art of this story; the graceful simplicity of the complex.

I continued in my musings. If Naomi is the ground of the meaning, she is also the ground of Being, she is the creative Place. As she creates the place/space she perforce undergoes the experiences of that place ... and ... because Naomi is the one who undergoes she therefore is the one who initiates. I found myself brought back to the beginning in a fine circle: the wheel of creating space and initiating action – but this time not as the Lone Naomi. Some weeks later I happily realized this thinking was in accordance with concepts in Kabbalah, when describing the S'firot Tree, therefore I shall return to these images in the sections dealing with that discipline.

A further round image: Naomi is the unwitting actor who nonetheless is the hub of the wheel, the pivotal point around which all transpires. And yet, not only is this biblical book not named for her, she is not counted in the grand throng of prophetesses.[7] Why?

Is it because Naomi does not enter the story proclaiming a mission? or because she is not consciously a reformer? But then neither is that the case with most of the prophetesses. Certainly Naomi's behavior is just the opposite to that of the impassioned prophets driven by God's command to effect change ... and not necessarily succeeding. Naomi *does* effect change, but not from a divine plan of action given to her at the outset. The change Naomi creates is by virtue of changes within herself.

The Hebrew word for prophet, *navi*, comes from an Akkadian word *nabu* meaning 'a call' and we have no mention in the story of Naomi's having received a calling from God. We

---

[7] According to legend the prophetesses in the Bible number eleven: Sara, Rebekah, Rachel, Leah, Miriam, Tamar, Bat-sheva, Abigail, Deborah, Hannah and Huldah.

do however have her declaration of being singled out by God: "The Lord has tormented me" ... or .... "born witness against me." Naomi's *sufferings* cause change. Changes in Naomi, in the story, in history, perhaps even changes in God's cognizance of the matter.[8]

Naomi's task and manner is just the opposite of the prophets.' Their task is to boldly go forth and speak to the people according to God's "outspoken" dictates. They stand apart from ordinary men. What's more, they are an *idealistic,* driven and impassioned lot. She, on the other hand, is the epitome of a conventional and obedient wife who obeys her husband and the traditions of her culture. At the same time she is not subservient, for even within her obedience she stands staunchly in her own truth. When life has turned bleak she blatantly states her bitter experience, *".... the hand of the Lord has struck out against me,"* and later, *"Call me Mara, for Shaddai has made my lot very bitter. I went away full, and the Lord has brought me back empty. ... the Lord has dealt harshly with me, ... has brought misfortune upon me."*

These are powerful statements of unjust punishment and Naomi bluntly lays the blame at the right doorstep – yet all the while she *accepts,* even within her bitterness and torments, the way things are. A woman unquestioningly embedded in her culture. There is something wonderfully realistic about her; matter-of-fact, down-to-earth. Her commitment to life, her compassion, her bitterness – all are equally *non-idealistic.* Natural.

With this word "natural" a gleeful and contriving imagination got the better of me. Was Naomi not gladly freed by the death of her binding chauvinist husband? In a flash I swept

---

[8] As we see later in the phrase "God took note of" (or "remembered") His people" – and – as is described by Jung (in a somewhat similar situation) in speaking of Job's unjust sufferings and the mirror this held up to God of His own unconsciousness. This is in keeping with the kabbalistic dialogue between man and God, and Jung's dialectic of Self and ego, seen in religious terms as God needing man.

aside all I had meticulously seen to be true of the character of
Naomi as I indulged in following a subjective fantasy – and a
popular trend. I actually allowed myself to go so far as to
greedily look for the Nature Woman in the Natural Naomi! I
forced my childhood vision of the mother in the fields into a
modern mold of romantic feminism as I sniffed around
eagerly for the independent runner with the wind ... the
woman who lifts up her skirts and runs with the wind for the
sheer hell of it. True, such an image would satisfy my natural
proclivities but the minute I viewed it I laughed aloud at my
lie. Naomi is nothing if not self-contained and conventional.
And therein lies her strength.

What does this say about me and my culture that such an
image could thrust itself so cheerily upon my sensibilities? Are
so many of us so overburdened with civilization? I must return
to this later.

Naomi's instinct is every bit as instinctual as the primitive
nature woman, but it is more in the mode of Protectress of the
Culture. If I were to place her into any one of our cherished
pantheon of archetypal images it would be that of priestess to
the women in their initiation rites ... and even this is forced,
ready-made and out of context as it is.

It is far more accurate to see Naomi as Everywoman,[9]
ordinary and extraordinary. She reflects our manifest emotional realities, our times of delight and despair. Hers is the
image to encourage our courage to suffer life fully and fulfill
our destiny. As Everywoman she becomes the very key to
innovation. Paradoxically, the innovations spring from her
traditional woman's way. They come about neither by a
calling nor by a dream, promise or vision (as they do with the
prophets). Naomi is quite alone. She has no revelation. God

[9] This phrase for Naomi sounded happily familiar to me and I remembered it was
used by Lois C. Dubin in her interesting article from the collection *Reading Ruth*
(ed. Kates and Reimer, New York, 1994).

does not speak to her. In fact, God does not speak at all in this story … at least, not out loud.

CHAPTER 3

Drought and the Journey Back

When Elimelech decided to leave for green pastures did Naomi and the boys regret leaving their friends and home? Did their friends resent them for copping out during hard times? There's no doubt that Naomi is of noble character, and according to the *Midrash Rabbah* even of noble birth … but surely this didn't rule out doubts and fears. Was Naomi not filled with foreboding on entering an alien territory? a land whose inhabitants had been her people's enemy and who still were forbidden to them in marriage? Furthermore, how did the family of Elimelech go such a distance by themselves? Did they take a trade route traveling by camel and donkey? Were there inns along the way? Did they welcome the welcoming hosts of Bedouin encampments? Dodge the fierce marauders who frequented trade routes? There was no question but to obey him whose name is "My God is King," but …

I know something of the way from Bethlehem to Moab. A descending route from the hills of Judea, it is lowland hilly and all desert with occasional oases. I find it vastly beautiful but I cannot imagine a journey across it by foot or by beast without conjuring up some of the hardships of Exodus, albeit an exodus in reverse; eventually arriving at the River Jordan but crossing it in the opposite direction – a regression in service of progression, as our text has it – backwards/forwards to the land of the goddesses. The rough road back, down the rocky terrain of the Judean Hills, to the desert, traversing the valley of the Jordan Rift, crossing that river, the up hills again into fertile Moab, to sit in the lap of the goddess in the land where she was not subdued.

Not that the goddess could ever truly be subdued! "A land flowing with milk and honey" is the goddess herself, that being her food as well as the food from her. It could be said that with the advent of an invisible masculine God in heaven, land became goddess – or rather, since land always was – that it remained goddess while woman lost that value. The new religion of sheer spirit took all the glory of Her out of the woman-body. After so many centuries land became disembodied. Mother Nature took her revenge and the land "naturally" grew dry. Famine ensued. The experience of Woman was once more called upon to flesh out spiritual principle.

These days we have returned to, or perhaps we never completely left, the drought caused by the absence of the fertility goddess. Outer events may or may not be the same as in our story, but the same archetypal principle is operating in modern men and women suffering from lack of the bountiful feminine presence.

We speak of people lacking a good relation to their feelings as being "too dry." Too dry and too rigid. More often than not we have used that expression for men, especially men who rely staunchly on principle in place of heart. I have had comical images of watering such men with the household watering can. In my practice however I have seen this drying up process taking place at least as frequently in women, women who are removed from their unique, individual femininity – due to a variety of circumstances, usually taking root early in life. Such women have lacked sufficient mothering appropriate to their needs and therefore are not at home with their woman-selves. Whatever the specific cause the resulting problem is a one-sidedness that is not 'at home' in the Mother – and this lack is abundant in our day.

Sometimes women raised with such one-sidedness are well adapted to those qualities associated with the masculine. They are cool clear ladies who don't show their emotions, not even to themselves. Ice Queens. Such clear-headed adaptation to Reality may have granted them a large degree of success – outwardly. Inwardly we find the old story of a lonely and hungry person, suffering from a famine in her land. On a more obviously dramatic level they are women whose bodies actually do dry up; they stop having their menstrual period and/or have a dry vagina, making sexual intercourse painful – as the acts of love-loss have been toward them.

It is as if their femininity has gone on strike, demanding greater pay. Sometimes it is a hunger strike resulting in a gaunt appearance that articulates their inner state; or the flip side of the coin, they indulge in frantic bouts of over-eating to gain their substance, or they water themselves with drinking, seeking therein the spirits they feel lacking. Other times they pay their dues in indiscriminate sexuality, or (again conversely) frigidity, being fearful of touch. Attitudes toward mothering are greatly effected here, as can be appreciated considering that the problem has arisen from absence of adequate mothering, either from the personal mother or from outer circumstance – environmental drought. Again this can appear as a coin of two sides: on one side there is a fear of mothering, on the other, a tremendous need to fill the gap by longing to be a mother in order to shower her baby with the love she herself was denied (thereby receiving love in return). A child who is the result of such conception experiences that hungry love, however subtly, as lack of personal loving and understanding. Thereby the problem as such continues, and thus the coin may continue to roll from generation to generation. Naturally this effects relationships, as one either longs for or rejects (sometimes both simultaneously, as there is a strong ambivalence) in the other, that which has been undeveloped in one's' own life.

These all too sketchy examples are illustrative of unconscious attempts to approach or even placate the fertility
goddess of grains – as well as taking her into themselves.
Indiscriminate sex may be voiced as "freedom" but it acts very
much as a frantic search for eros, unconsciously *reenacting* the
ancient orgiastic rituals held in honor of the love goddess.
When starving themselves, it is as if in spiteful *defiance* of the
goddess who has neglected them, or perhaps it is *mourning* for
her, and with her, as in Demeter's bereavement in the ritual
fasting in the Eleusinian Mysteries. The longing to be the
love-showering mother may be an attempt to heal herself
through *identifying* with the goddess. Yet another mode is in
replacing, to sit in the lap of the goddess by finding her in a
woman lover.[10] These (and more) complex turnings of life are
expressions on a personal level of a famine that is described in
such sparse narrative in the first chapters of the Book of Ruth.

It should be remembered – as it was in our text – that the
mother-goddess and the love-goddess return through genuine
acts of love and focused (i.e. conscious) yearning. Not hungry-
love, though starvation may indeed be the impetus. This
focused yearning allows for a return which is a *new* turn ...
which indeed might never have happened had it not been for
the initial loss of her. Woman *and* goddess – as well as the
woman's relationship to the masculine – are all transformed in
this Return[11].

The entry of the positive Mother perforce includes that of
the Father, and vice versa. We sometimes forget that these
principles, Mother and Father, are utterly interdependent.
One cannot exist without the other, even if the value given
and/or received is not equal. Following are a couple of modern

[10] These are scant examples and not equations. Any mode of behavior is far more
complex than a reduction to a sad neediness would allow.
[11] These dynamics can richly be seen in the Hebrew word for "return": "t'shuva"
which also has the meaning of "repentance" or "penitence" as well as "answer"
and is associated in Kabbalah with the s'fira Binah, also called "the upper
mother."

examples of the problem of psychological drought. Though not of the same events as in the story of Ruth they reflect the same inner problem of drought due to absence of the goddess.

A woman in her late 20's, born into a conventional middle-class environment, suffered from an absent father and an ineffectual mother who was no equal to her daughter's spiritedness. Since the absent personal father left room for the archetypal father to enter, and since such psychic reality had no humanizing mediation, this woman experienced *The Father* writ large! In this case the daughter suffered from an overabundance of strict patriarchal dictums. These dictums she experienced as severe social constraints which she projected onto society's rules and regulations. She had no personal father who would recognize her unique feminine qualities and be delighted by them, nor did she have a mother (erroneously seen as stupid and weak) who could nurture this nature that was so different from her own. With this lack of appropriate parenting the young woman was psychically orphaned. She wanted badly to be held and loved but she exhibited that need by displaying a defiant attitude toward life and bourgeois society in outrageous thumbing-her-nose actions. She was anorexic, she dressed like a frightening clown, picked fights, and had sex at the slightest provocation, even with strangers. She complained bitterly and frequently of her dry vagina, seeing in it her curse and her punishment.[12] She had gone dry. She no longer had her period and, not surprisingly, she couldn't cry. The famine was certainly in her land. Eyes, womb and vagina ... her centers and expressions of feeling ... had gone dry. Beneath her forced mask of defiance it was not hard to see a frightened child – nor hard to see an

---

[12] The "absent" personal mother leaves room for the entry of the archetypal, either positive or negative; in this instance entering as Witch-like Destiny. Cf. also Erich Neumann's *The Child* where guilt is explained in terms of disturbance of the primal relationship to the mother: "... that not-to-be-loved is identical with being abnormal, sick, 'leprous,' and above all, 'condemned'." p. 86 (New York 1973)

artistic and intelligent woman with a warm and vulnerable heart. I gave her a lot of loving mothering, but in my fashion, which could empathize with her distaste for many of society's norms and could mirror her feisty wit – a trait lacking in her natural mother. The day I impulsively picked her up and rocked her on my lap (an act which came as much of a surprise to me as it did her) began her ability to cry. She cried and cried and all I could do was to hold her and rock her like a baby. She told me gratefully, wistfully, that I smelled like her mother; the first positive toning about her mother she ever expressed.

Despite the touching depth of the moment I could not help but wonder what her mother smelled like. Her tone however was so lovingly longing that I could only interpret it as something positive. Also, the sense of smell being so animal-like, lent the feeling of something very primary being stirred in her. After that came the following dream, deceptively simple:

She dreamed that her father had returned and they were sitting in her childhood home; he in a comfortable armchair and she on his lap. She was her current age in the dream. They were sitting by a large window. They hugged one another, she was happy, and she cried and cried. She could visualize that inside of her vagina there were hundreds of little eyes, all crying, wet with tears. The lamp by the chair goes off and she notices the view out the window. The sun is bright ... and shining on a vast field of wheat.

I would say that experiencing positive mothering with me (on a level of early childhood), evoked the return of the father, thereby allowing this woman her own emotions, her own qualities of feminine and erotic moisture which touched her wounded love and by which she gained a new consciousness (*view*, and *light* from the *sun*, and *eyes* in her vagina) of Mother Earth (field of grain). It's interesting that in the dream the father is personal and the mother abstract, and that the "personal" light goes out in order to see the larger view.

After this incident and dream she established a warm relationship with the mother and began taking better care of her body, her dress, and her home. The father was still out of the picture but the negative projections diminished, as did the sexual acting out. Her outer appearance changed dramatically to what one would call a "normal" person – and a very attractive one at that. The doorway to knowing herself had begun to open.

I make this purposely brief for I don't intend to go into dream interpretation though it is tempting to do so. The dream itself shows primarily a compensating and reassuring relation to her lost father – by which she gained better relation to the mother and the feminine; therefore we could be justified in seeing this as a father problem ... which it also was. However, as I stated above, the archetypes of the Mother and the Father are interdependent. Also, this woman's personal anger at her mother as well as her lack of accepting her own woman's body and emotions, is tied initially to problems with the mother, the person from whose woman-body she emerged and from which she received sustenance. I feel justified therefore in using this as an example of the redeeming power of the "positive mother returned" and all that returns with her.

This illustration is connected to the book of Ruth where the masculine (as Boaz) is both the redeemer-protector of the feminine (Naomi/Ruth) as well as the redeemed. This new relation to the masculine, in fact the new masculine image in itself, would not have come about had it not been for Naomi receiving Ruth's cleaving to her, and Ruth's following Naomi's guidance.

This dreamer presents a somewhat gaudy example in comparison with the discretion of the Book of Ruth, but another example following the theme of dryness, is quieter.

A young bride came to work with me. She suffered from terrible heart pains for which no specialist could find a cause. She had little intimate connection to her mother, which was a lack during this time in her life where she would have done well to know something of the woman's ways. She was closer to her father and her outlook was decidedly rational. As with the former dreamer she carried ready-made attitudes toward society, but in the opposite direction: she was very obedient to rules and regulations. She was trying with all good will to adjust to the new land of married life as she was "supposed to," but will alone wasn't working. She didn't cry – not because she couldn't but because she didn't allow herself to be so childishly emotional, or in her terms, "unfair." She spoke coolly and intelligently of sad things, which sadness she either immediately undercut by statements such as, "Even in the best of marriages …" or relativized with comparisons to the worlds' suffering. She seemed to me to be a sacrificial victim – perhaps to her father – but to what purpose we had yet to learn. During one session, in response to her speaking from a point so high above her immediate emotions, and seeing her eyes deepen, my eyes teared up in sympathy. This was enough to release her tears … and to bring the sadness to a more personal level, from which she then spoke.

The following session she came in with a brief dream. She was at her in-laws' and the territory was all parched and dry with deep cracks in it due to a long drought. This did not surprise her considering her feelings of and for these people. I, or some older woman, come to visit her there and while conversing with her outdoors it begins to rain and the earth begins to soften. Soon they are standing in a field of grass.

*
* *

Yes, I know something of the way from Bethlehem to Moab. Living in Jerusalem, close to the town of Bethlehem, I often made trips from there to the Dead Sea, Eastwards towards what was Moab and is now part of Jordan, on the other side of the river. I too would go seeking renewal. Whenever I felt too pressured and living under God's thumb I would make a pilgrimage down to the Ancient Mother of the Dead Sea, pitch my orange pup tent and camp out by her side.

I know the rough and dry terrain. It may have been greener in the days of the Bible but it couldn't have been less rough and rocky, less descending. Down, down, down to the lowest spot on earth. Down from the Judean Hills to the desert, to the caves in the cliffs of Qumran and the hills of Ein Gedi by the shores of the Dead Sea[13] … to the land where the clear air and sweet smells tickle the nose; to the land where the ancient stories tell us that demons danced and goddesses roamed.

---

[13] *Yam haMelech* = "Salt Sea" in Hebrew, so salten that no marine life lives in it, therefore called "dead," though it is abundant with minerals, and people come from around the world to float in it and be "healed."

CHAPTER 4

Excursions into Names of Places
and the Place of the Desert

They still do dance and roam there, those demons and goddesses. The goddess's goats – sinning, redeeming and luring with singing – the Lilit screech owl, her fiery serpents and scorpions, and the wild ibex. All are abundant in that area. Even the leopard is making her come-back. The buff, gold and orange of the desert cliffs whose colors shift with the shifting sun and moon, the hard and thorny land which surprises us suddenly with oases of fresh springs, hidden falls, pools and springtime flowers ... all this has the wild gentle feel of 'primal feminine.'

This feeling of the feminine is not only a subjective fancy of mine. I have found it recognized by many who are not prone to personalizing landscapes in this way. The feminine quality of the Negev and Dead Sea desert is especially noticeable when compared to the desert of the majestic Sinai, some miles to the south and west. There one is awed by the steep and overpowering mountains so sharp and silver. At the foot of, and climbing, Mt. Sinai I am more "ecstatic" than "whole" in myself; more moved by the spirit than soothed by the soul. The wondrous feel of the Sinai is sheer masculine spirit and it is not at all surprising that the awesome, invisible, masculine God made Himself known there. It is however some 3 or 4 centuries later that the opposite revelation had to be reacquired, and we find the gold and buff, the rounded desert hills, to be the setting where the family of Elimelech must journey in their return to know the goddess.[14]

In Biblical and earlier times land was most certainly personalized, or rather divinized, and we often see place names referring to the local god or goddess, or to that experience therein. See how Jacob names the place of his dream, "Bet El," (House of God) for "This is none other than the abode of God, and that is the gateway to heaven."[15] He dreamed of a ladder connecting heaven and earth on which angels ascended and descended. Places are not only inhabited by God (or whatever local spirit) but 'place' and 'god' are part and parcel of the same reality. In Judaism even the word "place" (*haMakom*) is sometimes used with the mystical meaning of "God," the place/presence of God ... and as Presence it would be the Sh'chinah, the feminine presence of God. Towns not buried under by modernity are palpably experienced as spirited by the ancient gods or goddesses ... and often even modernity can't dampen the spirit. Just see how in the land we suppose to be solely of "patriarchal" bent many place names still reveal a feminine presence.

The southernmost tip of Israel is in the form of a triangle (itself an icon of the feminine) and this points to a desert port town by the Red Sea. This beautiful triangle is the meeting point of mountain, desert and sea, as well as a tripartite meeting point of Israel, bounded on either side by Egypt and Jordan. In this abundance she is called simply, "Goddess," *Eilat*. A lush area in the southerly central part of Israel is called the "Valley of the Goddess," *Emek Ella*. My home in a Jerusalem neighborhood is an enchanting place with winding,

---

[14] In our Western imagination, specifically in alchemy, white and silver is the color of the feminine (moon) and red or gold (sun) is the masculine. This is sometimes the opposite to a system in Kabbalah where white is the color of the masculine (semen) and red is the color of the feminine (blood).

[15] Genesis 28:16-20

hidden streets and inner courtyards, which also retains its biblical name, *Emek Refa'im,* "Valley of the Ghosts." In the light of our daily business we live in the midst of these ancient fantasies. In some areas the light of the fantasy bounds with greater clarity, as the Dead Sea's *Ein Gedi,* which in itself means the "Spring of the Goat" ("spring" as water), not a god or goddess but certainly the animal of the goddess as well as a *daimon* in its own right, as well as the inhabiting animal in that desert place. *Se'ir* in Hebrew, "hairy one," means both "goat" and "demon." As we know, whether this creature is considered demon, devil or god depends upon the fantasy of the religion in which it is viewed.

Lilit (Lilith), that lamia so many women want to love and glorify these days, pranced about in the desert birthing hundreds of demon children per day in non-discriminating, boundless fertility, bound to produce bounding demons. It should be remembered that this heroine of self authority has no milk in her breasts to nurse her children – unlike the abundantly nursing *Anata,* the goddess of Cana'an. Anata also remains with us.

Today as in biblical times, a town on the outskirts of Jerusalem (entering the desert our characters traversed) is called by the name of Anata. Now she is an Arab town. In the Bible she was the prophet Jeremiah's home and called Anatot, the plural of Anata.[16] How appropriate for the impassioned prophet – proclaiming the Lord's way to the wayward Jews worshipping the Queen of Heaven, Ashera[17] – to be living in her daughter's town. The town remembers that and so do we, its visitors, when Jew and Arab meet there – sometimes one, sometimes the other, taking the role of the Just Jeremiah or the Fertile Anata. There is need for both these characters …

---

[16] Goddesses names were sometimes pluralized since the goddess was seen in her dual aspect as mother and maiden, such as Demeter and Persephone or for that matter, Naomi and Ruth.

[17] Ashera [also Ashtarot, Astarte, linked to Ishtar] is the mother of Anata.

and what a union that could make! That union is what the Book of Ruth is about.

We get stuck in our habitual ways of thinking ... which is also a drying up process. All that rigidity gets loosened in the sifting sands of the desert where opposites turn into one another and mirage is reality. The desert is a paradoxical place, or so it appears to our conscious minds, for it is opposite to our habitual existence and animated with spirits who eerily dance about confusing our known boundaries of ugly and beautiful, of good and evil, while exhibiting both qualities in bold relief. It is a liminal place *par excellence.* As such it is an apt metaphor for entry into the unconscious.

Just listen to the ancient happenings of this desert wilderness where the family of Elimelech traversed toward Moab, and see how it is the right setting for the entry into their fate of death and rebirth:

This goat-footed demon/daimon land is a theatre for the torments and the cleansing of the soul. In the days of the Temple, on Yom Kippur (Day of Atonement) an identical pair of goats was placed before the High Priest (descendent of Aaron) who cast lots to determine their separate fates. One goat became the burnt offering to God, sacrificed upon the altar of the Temple. The other goat became the offering to Azazel, an ancient demon of the desert whose name became synonymous with Satan. The High Priest would put his hand upon this goat's head and with prayer lay all the sins of the people of Israel onto this one animal, who was then led into the desert to be left there; sent into the desert to Azazel.[18] One goat to God, the other to Azazel.

This special goat came to be known in English as the "scapegoat."[19] We feel sadness for this creature whose name has come to mean a person or nation who is made to carry the unjust evil projections of others. This is a misunderstanding of

[18] Cf. Rivkah Schärf Kluger, *Satan In the Old Testament,* pp. 41 – 48. (Northwestern University Press, 1967).

the role of this goat who was neither cast out unjustly nor as a punishment, but who was *chosen by God*[20] to carry and suffer the sins of the people[21] ... into the pristine wilderness, there to be transformed, carrying them to the barren wasteland, in the howling dessert, back to their origins.

My view of desert as origins and place of transformation is in accordance with the psychological and symbolic meaning of wilderness as the unconscious. Kabbalah also has this as the meaning of the desert where it is the realm of the *sitra achra*, the "other side." In Kabbalah it is the domain of Evil, being ruled by Sama'el and Lilit (the counterparts to God and his Sh'chinah). So, the sin-bearing goat is sent into sin's realm. The immediate interpretation in the Zohar is that the goat is an offering to appease the evil powers. However a further meaning, more in accordance with my statement of origins and transformation, has the quality of the desert explained by an old man dwelling with the hermits there:

> "'And in the desert where you have seen how the Lord your God bore you, as a man bears his son' (Deut. 1:31) ... The Holy One, blessed be He, led Israel into the desert, a terrible desert, as it is written 'serpents, fiery serpents and scorpions' ... He brought them out to journey in the terrible desert, which is the place where wicked Sama'el reigns ... And had not Israel sinned the Holy One, blessed be He, would have wished to remove him from the world. This is why He made them pass through his very own land, his portion, and his inheritance. ... And so we too (the hermit and his companions) have forsaken civilization for the

---

[19] The word "scapegoat" comes from a misunderstanding of the name Azazel as being a combination of two Hebrew words '*ez*' and '*ozel*,' meaning "escaped goat."

[20] Casting lots is abdicating individual will and choice in order to leave open the space for the hand of chance-destiny-God to come in.

[21] To sacrifice is to 'make sacred.' It is therefore 'holy,' which in Hebrew is '*kodesh*' (coming from a meaning to 'set apart,' i.e., from the mundane). The term used in Hebrew for sacrifice is '*corban*' meaning to 'draw near,' 'come close.' What we call the cut off, cast out part is in fact *drawn close* ... to God. The cast out portion is for the purpose of atoning – not for punishment and not for repression.

harsh wilderness, to study Torah there, in order to subdue this side. *Furthermore, it is only there that the words of Torah can be fully understood, for there is no light except that which proceeds from darkness ... And there is no worship of the Holy One, blessed be He, except that which comes from darkness, and there is no good except that which comes from evil. ..."*

Zohar II, 183b [italics mine]

The meaning is that Evil – which here is protected and granted by God – is not just for punishing, or only to be shunned, but is an experience that is part of, and causes, transformation – and to both sides. The study of Torah (God's teachings, enlightenments) *subdues* Sama'el, yet it is just *within* the domain of the evil powers of Sama'el that one can truly experience and gain the transforming effects of enlightenment. Gaining wholeness through the play of opposites, even redemption through sin, is central in Kabbalah. Highly psychological![22 & 23]

Desert as origins and place of transformation is also reflected in the following description of God finding the people Israel:

---

[22] "Redemption through sin" can be grossly misunderstood by a warped personality that takes the mystical and psychological idea literally and concretizes it in lewd and/or criminal acts; a flagrant violation of the laws of religious behavior, to which the kabbalists devoutly adhered. One famous example is Shabbtai Zvi, ... who had a complete antinomian approach to Kabbalah, in the name of redemption ... the false messiah of the 17th century, on whom Scholem has written the definitive study – of the man, his prophet, the kabbalah ... and an intricate study on the timeless problem of evil: *Sabbatai Sevi: The Mystical Messiah,* Princeton University Press, 1973

[23] The scapegoated person, as we use the term today, does have its connections with the original meaning of the sacrifice since that person carries the shadow of who it is that is doing the scapegoating ... and is thereby not only condemned by their accusers' conscious accusations but carries those unconscious, secret urges that are hoping to find *within* the victim their own redemption! This would be the redeeming aspect of the shadow. The wisdom of such dynamics lives in the unconscious ... and will remain there if the accuser remains stuck on vengeance ... or whatever is driving her/him to do the scapegoating.

He found him a desert land
In the howling waste of the wilderness:
He encircled him, watched over him
He guarded him as the apple of His eye.
Like an eagle who rouses his nestlings ...
So did He spread His wings and take him ...

(Deuteronomy 32:10-11)

Walking alone one dawn when I was 14, in the new light of the vast desert, I felt myself to be at the beginning of creation. I had arisen earlier than anyone else, except for the goats with whom I had a good morning's greeting. I continued on into this rocky desert wilderness to watch the new sun rising. I was at the very beginning of Time ... in utter stillness, in the hush of the soft morning wind. All was connected. Every object combined in itself body, soul and spirit – past, present and future. All was exquisitely interwoven and just beginning to unfold into a differentiated awesome Creation. Here in the desert one can, one must, remember origins ... as would a child, conscious of seeing and being seen for the first time.

Like grapes in the wilderness, I found Israel.
Like the first fruit on the fig tree, I saw your fathers.

(Hosea 9:10)

It is in this so-called barren landscape where one is privileged see the bare naked form of the spirit; the rocks, the fearful fullness of empty space.[24] It was at the mouth of a desert cave that Elijah heard God in the "small still voice," or as another translation has it, "a soft murmuring sound."[25]

Over 2 000 years ago the Essenes, living in Qumran, chose this desert by the Dead Sea in which to live in retreat (sometimes going forth to teach) in order to cleanse themselves and be prepared by their purity for the Millennium.

---

[24] In Hebrew the word "tsur" is the word for "rock" and also "form," The same root gives "yotser" as creator and The Creator; and "yotsrani" as "creative."
[25] *Tanakh, The Holy Scriptures*, Jewish Publication Society, Philadelphia, New York, Jerusalelm, 5748, 1988.

They lived a communal life, many of them an ascetic life, to receive anew the Torah from God, and to renew their Covenant ... as if in celebration of an ongoing Shavu'ot. A most spiritual place for them. Bare. Clean. Unadorned.

Actually the desert is beautifully adorned if one looks closely, but certainly not with the refinements of civilization. I become a crass conservative, or more accurately an impassioned Jeremiah, crying and pleading, warning those who bring the "comforts" of civilization into the wilderness – who dare even to make tourist spots of hotels there – of the disaster they are bringing about by their infidelity, "You are idolaters, blasphemers, sinners, calling damnation upon God's creation!" That's how strongly I feel about the pure and terrible beauty of this desert.

When I returned to Israel in 1979, after an absence of 20 years, I had recurrent dreams whose setting was on the banks of the Dead Sea, in that area of it which is abundant with weird salten forms, coagulated into eerie sculptures which rise from the sea and pose on the land. In the dream there was an *absolute* stillness. The only movement was mist coiling upward from the innards of the salten forms rising from the sea, as if miniature moist volcanoes. The mood was heavy with apocalyptic expectation. This was a border place, the End and Beginning of Time, as well as being the geographical border between Israel and Jordan. This was a place where Eternity chose to appear in the Moment. A fearful wondering filled me and though neither the word nor concept "messianic" appeared in the dream, the mood could only be described as burstingly pregnant with such. All was vast, empty, quiet. No person was there except for me and a bearded man of my age who was wise and spoke comfortingly to me. He assured me that I was right in knowing the mood and portent of the place, but that we needn't fear even though fearful times were near. In this spot there would eventually be peace between Jew and Arab – there would be a New Age.[26] This dream came a few times and though it well referred to my personal fears and hopes, it was no less an accurate description of a spooking, pregnant quality so present in that place. A place of borders, of borderline experiences, of death and renewal.

And so it must have been with the Essenes, with Jesus, with the early Christian Saints tested in the wilderness; a quality drawing the Greek Orthodox churches to perch precariously there on jagged mountain heights, a quality still spoken by the caves hosting wandering seekers of truth … and bats. Ein Gedi is where King David hid in a cave from a maddened King Saul … and was protected by a spider. A desert cave is where Elijah hid from evil King Ahab and was fed morning and evening by the ravens. Oh so many stories of desert spirit as wild sanctity and sanctuary … outside civilization … forever ancient, forever new.

And this is where the family of Elimelech traversed, backward/forward.

The trip in our story is a regression, as our text explains, but not one based on wish-fulfilling gratification's, though the Midrash Rabbah does accuse Elimelech of cowardly escaping his community's problems … which was my first take on the situation.[27] Then again, perhaps the Midrash Rabbah is correct in this explanation for it explains why it was that Elimelech didn't make it in Moab. In this midrash death is a punishment for Elimelech's cowardice, as it is in the Zohar Ruth, where Elimelech is a "leader of his generation but escapes from their plight." In our text Elimelech's death is interpreted symbolically as the necessary dying of the old

---

[26] For me, and most living in Israel, the meaning of peace between Arab and Jew is more than a rational political event. If not what most would call "messianic" it nonetheless carries such atmosphere, the tremendous psychological weight of a resolution of opposites that have been warring in the soul of the land and its people for millennia. Also, since most consider this "holy land" such peace represents the longed for universal peace promised in religions.

[27] Cf. Rashi's (1040-1105 France) commentary on the Book of Ruth and his interpretation of Elimelech's departure, also as in the Midrash, Ruth Rabbah (circa 6th century C.E.).

ruling principle, which makes space for the new, while the sons' deaths are the outcome of the power of the feminine which overwhelms the young masculine. This last interpretation is psychological while the others are moral, with the Zohar Ruth being allegorical as well as moral. All these modes are apt as ways and means of understanding that trip made backwards/forwards into the realm of the great goddess. They may also serve as styles descriptive of entry into the unconscious.

How one enters the unconscious (as well as the desert) can determine the outcome. "Am I taking it seriously?" "Am I strong enough?" "Am I able to forgo habitual ways and means in order to humbly wonder at new realities?" or, "Am I running away from the drought and dirth of everyday life, seeking escape into The Wonders?" "Am I glib and intellectually facile in interpreting the images?.."

Even if one does have the correct attitude for entry into the unconscious there is little choice, if the journey is to go forward, but to be faced with shadows, to allow to die that which must die and to bear the unexpected twists and turns of fate – with devotion, receptivity, love and curiosity. A genuine *amor fati*. A genuine feminine attitude of acceptance of one's destiny.

It is in all these ways of traversing the desert that I've come to understand the journey of the Family Elimelech from Bethlehem in Judah down to Moab, on the "Other Side." The necessary descent. Rough, rocky and dry, sometimes barren or filled with fear, sometimes the oases in settings that promise the goal. In this way we all know something of the journey from Bethlehem to Moab.

CHAPTER 5

Seeking the Goddess

In its first five lines the Book of Ruth carries us on a swift trip: an introduction to the family of Elimelech, their departure from Bethlehem, the journey to Moab, the death of Elimelech, the marriage of Machlon and Chilion to Moabite women and the death of those boys! I wondered at first if so little elaboration is given due to the fact that in times of drought or bitterness images tend not to flow – or is it rather not the case that the bare bone events boldly reveal the essential reality? The impact of the essence can be hindered by details. Nonetheless my curiosity constantly shifts between the symbolic and the concrete, between essential and supplemental; two realities side by side and intertwining. I want to know what this distant relative of mine actually went through as a flesh and blood woman. I remain gross when compared with the terse subtlety of the biblical story.

Was Naomi somehow secretly gratified to be in the land where the fertile love goddess was openly revered? Surely Ruth and Orpah had household idols, *teraphim*, goddesses by the hearth. Once married and living in Naomi's home were those idols and their rituals left behind?[28] Perhaps not? How much adaptation took place between the women? My fantasy is that Naomi as the strong matriarch had a compassion which did not want to uproot her new daughters too roughly from their

ways. Their love for her indicates as much. Would she have
gone so far as to participate in their rituals?

Such ritual could not have been unknown to Naomi. In
Judah – as we know later from the anguished cry of the
prophets, as well as from current archeological evidence –
Jewish men and women made "Asheras" out of stone and
wood and celebrated in the ritual of burning incense to, and
baking cakes for, the Queen of Heaven – fertile Ishtar, Ashera,
Ashtarot – and participating in her orgiastic rites. As I have
said, the goddess could never really be out of the picture. As a
psychic reality, be it called mother, anima or goddess, she is a
fact of life not capable of disappearance. "Honor" however is
another matter quite capable of disappearance and in the new
masculine/spiritual religion, the goddess was no longer hon-
ored. To some degree, Nature and Spirit found themselves in
opposing camps. The goddess's rituals of open and mass
sexuality to insure fertility were prohibited as licentious idol
worship. It was not only particular practices that were forbidden (as voiced by the prophets), she was, in her entirety,
thought of as foul. Such casting out of the primal feminine,
the woman's soul image in the divine realm, may be even more
injurious to women than their being physically subjugated or
cast out. "You are here but your soul is not seen; you must live
in accordance with the new masculine spirit, not the old
feminine nature." Just imagine the bind if included in body
but not valued in principle!

Well, we don't have to imagine. Being "only an object" is
the woman's cry of our century. In our day we have come to
acknowledge just how damaging the denigration of the feminine can be. When we are left without our reflection in the

---

[28] It is only in recent generations that the newlyweds go forth to a home outside the
parents'. In Israel today it is not too uncommon for the Arabs, or for the
Sephardim (Jews hailing from Mediterranean regions or Arab countries), to
continue the tradition of adding apartments on to the "homestead" where the
newlyweds live, honoring "The Mother and The Father."

divine realm it is as if body and soul don't meet – it is as if "our fullness had been emptied." To whom then and to what can we turn to give us full reality, full dignity? Without full reality we find ourselves participating in a society (inner as well as outer) which has become tyrannical and binding ... despite having thrown away our corsets long ago. In such squeezed consciousness both men and women are victims, tied down, and tying down others, in bondage to their respective well-defined roles, whatever they may be, in whichever society lacks the gifts of a bountiful, bending, goddess.[29]

We have seen how, in an outworn society, people become stereotypes, flat remnants of a former archetypal reality, identified with one of its poles or the other such as the oft cited madonna/whore polarity. More commonly I've heard, "I am a wife and a mother, therefore I cannot return to school," or "to work," or, "I cannot have a room of my own." Fortunately this is not nearly so prevalent as it was 100 years ago ... 50 years ago ... yesterday? ... but it certainly still exists, even in emancipated, liberated women. At the same time, we have seen in this past century an increasing pervasion of values being turned upside-down and inside out. Women have made a point of leaving hearth and home, of worshipping the Black Goddess, of even having unnecessary hysterectomies, all in the name of individual identity and freedom. As in the old Cole Porter song of the early '30's "Anything Goes," going (perhaps) further than he imagined. That happy tune may have had its outcome in the youth-wail, "I've Gotta Be Me" of the '60's generation, though "me" is still, by and large, floating in amniotic fluid somewhere in future space. In the midst of this upheaval some cherish chaos in and for itself, while others understand it as the necessary labor pains heralding a new

---

[29] I am not arguing against the *necessity* of the masculine spirit overthrowing an overweening feminine spirit. ... as explicated in our text. I am speaking rather of the ensuing one-sidedness of the masculine, or of any dominant consciousness, once it has run its (necessary) course.

birth. Judaism and Christianity call such a time the "sufferings of the messiah" according to the belief that before Redemption there is a tremendous world-suffering.

Whether or not we buy the traditional view of the messiah as a bearded man, we do share that traditional image. Consciously such image does not irk me at all, yet my unconscious apparently wanted me to regain some concept of Messiah as Feminine for I had the following dream about 18 years ago:

> *I am in a kibbutz[30] and a group of us, having just finished our labors in the fields, are singing and dancing in a circle. In the midst of this happy circle dances a woman in her late fifties. She is a stocky-chunky, ordinary looking woman, in a most wholesome way. She is wearing the standard cotton shorts and blouse and she is barefoot. We stop our dancing to watch her and clap our hands in rhythm to her dance. She stops dancing a moment to remove a thorn from her foot. A voice says, "This is the Messiah."*

The image of "Woman Removing A Thorn From Her Foot" is a motif in Indian art, and perhaps is similar in meaning to an ancient Egyptian image where the thorn is symbolic of the mother-goddess Neith. I have not found why 'the thorn' but can only guess it is because the thorn and the flower go together as opposite sides of a single reality such as a rose – that single reality also being a part of all the plants of the earth, ruled by the mother goddess. Then again it could be the symbol of the "most perfect" (the Self, union of opposites), as the rose – the thorn being the most profane, the blossom the most sublime.

---

[30] A kibbutz is the collective, communal farm of modern Zionism arising from similar cooperative settlements established in Israel at the turn of this century. Their ruling principle was a work ethic of farming, believing that redemption of the land, in which every man and woman shared equally, was the redemption of one's own soul, as members of the Community of Israel. The members were known for their idealistic, non traditional, progressive education and "free thinking," which often included their acceptance of "free love."

This brings to mind the thorn bush in the Bible as the place of revelation, of God's declaring Himself to Moses as sheer Being, "I am/shall be that which I am/shall be." According to the rabbinic interpretations, it is the Sh'chinah as thornbush for whom Moses must remove his shoes, in order to receive Her ... barefoot and thorny. In Christianity the Savior wears the crown of thorns in his final sufferings, the passion which is followed by his rising to the sublime. In the Kabbalah the sufferings of the messiah are very much connected to the Sh'chinah for she suffers for and with the people. What's more, it is only through her that redemption will come. She is the mediatrix between God and humanity. According to Kabbalah "all women live in her shadow" (or, "her secret," "her mystery"). The Sh'chinah is reflected in and by all women and nature, down to the simplest person, and the humblest thorn bush. In the Zohar's interpretation of the Song of Songs it is the Sh'chinah who is both the thorn and the rose.

A further amplification for the dream is that the Sh'chinah is identified with the *Knesset Isra'el*, the Community of Israel. This brings the kibbutz into the picture, for the idea of redeeming the Community of Israel (the Jewish people) through Nature, through loving care of the land – which also was in need of redemption and *by* which oneself was redeemed, by land, by labor, by love – was an idea central to modern Zionism, beginning with the 1880's and gaining full articulation in the kibbutz movement. Many people gave up everything in their lives to work the land during the day and sing and dance to its beauty through the night. My father, at the age of 20, left his medical studies in New York (both he and my mother left comfortable homes there) in order to join a kibbutz, live in tents, eat nothing but "kasha" (buckwheat) and work arid land into fertility with a fervor that can only be called religious. A very earthy and so-called atheistic (as most kibbutzim declared themselves to be) religion. The kibbutzim, atheistic and spartan, is where the Chief Rabbi of Israel, the

famous kabbalistic mystic, Rav Kook, went for retreats.
Despite his strict orthodoxy he understood the spirit of the
kibbutz and declared, "They are doing the work of bringing in
the Messiah."[31]

It is not farfetched therefore to see in this dream the
Sh'chinah in her messianic role – shining in the humble and
healthy *kibbutznikit*[32] – removing the thorn (the "realm of the
husks" in Kabbalah[33]) from her foot.

Suffering as such is not in this joyful dream but the pricking
thorn is there and certainly the image of woman as redeemer
is; a very earthy, nature oriented messiah. Although the dream
was calling for my attention to own my own origins and goals,
it is also an image that suits our times, reminding and assuring
us that nature woman even (or especially) in her simplest
work-a-day guise belongs to that wonder we call messianic.

Surely Ruth, under Naomi's instructions to glean in the
fields, is an image of the humble, nature living woman who
through her labors becomes the instrument of redemption
and the vessel for the future Messiah. Furthermore, as we
recall from our text, Ruth carries the light of the Sh'chinah.
She is God's "lost dove," found in the land of Moab, in the
realm of the Other Side.

*
* *

Even if a redeeming virtue is simplicity, the way to redemption is not simple and we would hardly choose the sufferings
that lead to it. "Call me Mara" Naomi says; "Call me Bitter,"
referring to her suffering the sacrifices imposed upon her. Her
experience is so bereft of grace that she cannot any longer carry
her name "Naomi" as "my sweetness, my pleasure, my grace."

---

[31] I am speaking of the early days. There have been many changes and many
disappointments, though much of the beauty and 'honest' idealism remains.
(Rabbi Abraham Isaac Kook, 1865 – 1935)

[32] Female member of a kibbutz.

[33] The husks are the fallen part of Creation, that which is furthest from the Divine,
but nonetheless carries the remnant of creation, the divine spark within.

Her former identity as such has died with the deaths of her husband and sons. Or so she feels it.

"So the woman was left, without her two sons and without her husband." Of this Naomi says, "I went away full and I came back empty." A bitter experience. Tragic.

Are you remembering the *tragoidia*? – the satyr chorus of early Greek Tragedy arising from the dithyramb in the Dionysian festivals, referring to the *tragos,* the sacrificial goat? Our desert goat returns to my attention. Goats as sacrificial victim, the offering to Azazel, the song of the goat, the spring of the goat, the sexy goat, the milking goat, the god goat and devil as goat, the suffering sin-burdened goat – nature bound, bounding goat – the goat laughing at our dichotomy of instinct and spirit. All is interwoven in a lively background tapestry of this story, picturing a place of nature, transformation and inclusiveness.

Any true transformation, any urge toward birthing consciousness, can be chaotic and includes a birth of tragedy, even when not appearing with such global magnificence as described by Nietzsche. It carries its own kind of torment for it is tantamount to being dismembered. Torn apart from one's known identity, torn from "home," the upheaval of making the tortuous, unsure journey into foreign territory where one's ruling principle dies. A sacrifice of all that has been familiar. In our story it is Naomi who is the bearer of this suffering – which later is born as the means of redemption for her people.

We suffer our individual changes and transformations as well as suffering the transformation process of our current chaotic era – of which we are also the instruments. We suffer truly if we will bear the load. Because *how* we suffer determines the outcome, a distinction should be made in judging cries of victimization. Is this suffering caused by an urge "heaving its way toward Bethlehem"?, still unborn, still unknown, good or evil? – or is it caused by too much obedience to an outworn system? Whichever way it is painful, but the first bears fruit if consciously accepted, while the second by itself causes drought and famine. When stuck in the second our cries are peevish rather than being the real called for agony, the Greek *agon* as contest with the gods, wrestling as did Jacob with the Angel (or was it God Himself) when he strove all night on the banks of the river Jabbok in his life and death battle, finally being blessed at dawn with a new consciousness: his name as "Israel," "he who strives with God"... and bearing forever after the gifted wound.

We are all at the banks of God and Goddess Wrestling. Again. Jacob, ultimately the father of the twelve tribes of Israel, was still entering the new masculine spirit, especially in the light of his strong mother from whom he gained so much. Naomi had to strive in the opposite direction, back again to the strong mother. We are, at least collectively and historically, standing in the sandals of Naomi.

To reiterate our point: The pain of living under the new spiritual masculine religion did real damage to the feminine. According to R. Schärf Kluger the lack of the nature goddess is at the root of the barrenness of three of the four mothers of the Bible.[34] In their stories this is eventually remedied through conscious and loving acceptance of the new masculine spirit – which involved a sacrifice of their known ways – and the fruit that bore. This new consciousness then renews in turn a return of their feminine being; this time as instinct *united* with spirit. This is a dialectical process of suffering the conflict and tension of opposites which involves sacrifice of the old in the process of resolving the issue on a new level: a synthesis of the former opposition. A reconciliation of both in a brand new form.

---

[34] In Judaism there are three fathers, Abraham, Isaac and Jacob, and four mothers: Sara, Rachel, Leah and Rebekah. For an interpretation on the suffering and transformation of the biblical women see R.Schärf Kluger, "Old Testament Roots of Woman's Spiritual Problem" in *Psyche in Scripture* (Inner City Books, 1995) and our Y. Kluger text, chapter "Marriage and the Birth of a new *Go'el*"

Just as we must carefully judge our sufferings (to whom or what am I being victimized) so must we carefully make distinctions as to our sacrifice: To what purpose am I making this sacrifice? Are we sacrificing the old way in order to achieve the new – or are we sacrificing our integrity in order to appease society's norms? For instance, the sacrifice of Naomi (however non-willed by her) is of the first description where a teleological principle (or divine purpose, or process of individuation) is being followed, while the obedient new wife I told of in chapter 3 illustrates a sacrifice of the second kind which would have thwarted her future, had not she been "saved" by the older woman in the field.

Suffering chaos, being torn apart, transformation and synthesis – all of this I say in reference to honoring the goddess in a *conscious* dialogue. I believe It is exactly this *lack of consciousness* that is referred to in the prophets' crying out against the backsliding idolaters of the goddess. Those accounts do not point solely to the mistake of the masculine *not* recognizing the value of the feminine (as our feminist reading would have it), but of consciously *yes* recognizing the decay caused by being victims *unknowingly* (drawn backwards, backsliding), submitting to the power of an *unconscious* feminine force. After all, were the prophets' cries restrictive or imploring?

Was the adoration of the goddess (the baking of cakes for her, burning incense to her and participating in sexual rites) a psychological laxity of remaining in the past? – or a throwback due to a failure in living up to the new? – or a romantic longing to retrieve what had been lost? More positively, was it a realization of one's own base-nature *before* advancing to another level? We cannot know what it was for the individuals as individuals, but if we follow a theory that history "wants" to unfold toward greater consciousness, and if we allow that the Bible tells its stories sincerely, then we must consider the prophets' cries as calls for awakening rather than damnations.

Stirrings of the Sh'chinah

The worship of Ashera was eventually prohibited by King Josiah (about 700 B.C.E.) when he had her image removed from the Temple and forbade worship of her. But another feminine image, with particular Jewish qualities (I do not collapse distinctions between our great variety of goddesses) was to increasingly shine in the people's consciousness.

The New Moon ceremonies were always feminine in character, going back to the time of the Second Temple[35] (500 B.C.E.). Perhaps it was this eternal mode combined with the ever present qualities of goddess (forbidden or not) that gave rise to the continually evolving image of the Sh'chinah. The Presence makes one of her entrances, as we are told by the rabbis of old, when they said "whoever blesses the new moon is welcoming in the Sh'chinah."

It should be stressed that the Sh'chinah imagined as a separate entity grew only with time. However, even in the early days there were arguments among the Talmudists, in commenting on biblical passages, as to whether or not there was a distinct entity in the Sh'chinah – though always there was the defining characteristic of light and radiance. Originally, even though the word is feminine, the Sh'chinah referred only to the Divine Presence in the world, both the hidden and the manifest Immanence of God. However, already appearing in the 80's B.C.E. one finds a distinct personification and hypostasis of God's presence. In general such references spoke of God's nearness to man, i.e., "The Sh'chinah went before Israel and prepared a place for them to dwell in" and after the destruction of the Temple by Rome and the ensuing expulsion of Jews from Jerusalem it was written that the Sh'chinah "lifted herself from the land and accompanied Israel into exile." In the Talmud Rabbi Akiva interprets, "Wherever Israel was exiled, it is as if the Sh'chinah

[35] Encyclopedia Judaica, Keter Publishing House Jerusalem Ltd.

was exiled with them." Always the Sh'chinah is seen as a protecting agent, even if not drawing any distinction between God and Sh'chinah.

The correct reference to the Sh'chinah, then and now, is 'it' and never 'she,' keeping distinct the oneness of God. There is no separate existence, no divine 'he' or 'she' outside of God. All is seen as manifestations of qualities of God, later in Kabbalah as emanations of God. Still in all, and increasingly so in history, the name (Sh'chinah) came to be seen as a personification in its/her own right, standing apart from God and even arguing with Him in defense of the people to whom He was being harsh. (I therefore take the "incorrect" position of often saying "she" in honor of that quality being presented). This was taking place in the early days of the Talmud – beginning just before the current era. Today arguments still exist among scholars as to whether or not, at that early time, one could interpret the Sh'chinah as a created form, separate from God.[36] In those days all of the figurative references to the Sh'chinah as Princess, Bride, Mother and Matronita are not in use. Such identifications came into being with the Kabbalah.[37]

With the Kabbalists, notably in the Zohar of 13th century Spain, the Sh'chinah gained centrality in the process of God's creation and emanation, being quintessentially feminine and most definitely the mediatrix between holy and profane, the people and God. In her emanation as "Malchut" ("Kingdom") she is even sovereign of the world. The kabbalists of Ts'fat,[38] (Safed) in the Galil (Galilee), brought out even more intently the centrality and feminine qualities of the Sh'chinah

---

[36] The Medieval Jewish philosophers did speak of the Sh'chinah as a separate created entity, a sort of luminous body, but in so doing they broke the unity of God. The Kabbalists returned the Sh'chinah to her original meaning as part and parcel of God, with the addition being an emanation.

[37] For a thorough exposition on the Sh'chinah in early times see Ephraim E. Urbach, *The Sages; Their Concepts and Beliefs*, chap. III, The Magnes Press, The Hebrew University, Jerusalem, 1979

– her gifts of prophecy, love and fertility – focusing largely on a messianic meaning in Kabbalah. These mystics would, through meditation, ecstatic prayer and visions, welcome and receive the Sh'chinah; an ongoing quest to draw near to the Presence.

The Sabbath

"You shall call the Sabbath a Delight." (Leviticus 23:2) Kabbalah sees in this, "You should invite (call) the Sh'chinah (Sabbath) as a guest into your home – as a guest with a prepared table, wine and food."[39] The Sabbath is especially the time of the Sh'chinah, when the divine radiance fills the world and the profane is filled with the holy. Therefore preparations to receive the Sh'chianh were carefully attended to by the Ts'fat kabbalists. She was sought outdoors in the groves just before sunset and love songs were sung to welcome her. A song written by Solomon Alkabets in the 16th century: *"Lecha Dodi"* "Come my beloved, meet the Bride, Let us welcome Shabbat" is still sung in synagogues on Friday evening, the Sabbath eve. Included in the Sabbath ritual was the recital of the Song of Songs and Proverbs 31 ("A woman of valor who can find?"). These were intended as meditations on the Sh'chinah as God's mystical bride.[40] The Hassidim of 18th century Eastern Europe continued the kabbalists' emphasis on the Sh'chinah, bringing that esoteric mysticism into the streets, so to speak, and increasing the reverence of women as being vessels of the Sh'chinah. What many have not learned

[38] I refer particularly, but not only, to Isaac Luria, known as "ha-Ari," in the 16th century – the Lurianic Kabbalah.

[39] Isaiah Tishby, *The Wisdom of the Zohar, An Anthology of Texts,* Vol III p. 1286, The Littman Library, Oxford University Press, 1989.

[40] Gershom Scholem, *Kabbalah,* Keter Publishing House, Jerusalem, Ltd., 1974

these days is that there were even women rabbis among the early Hassidim![41]

On Shabbat, in antiquity as well as today, myrtle is often part of the ceremony. At *Havdallah* ("separation," the end of Shabbat, the moment when 3 stars can be seen in the sky), incense is burned, and/or sprigs of myrtle are smelled, in order to accompany with good smells, the holy back to the supernal realm, though it is also a good thing to draw out the Sabbath to persuade the Sh'chinah to linger longer – to allow the additional soul which one receives on Shabbat to remain, just a little while longer. "At the conclusion of Shabbat, when the additional soul departs, one must be refreshed by smelling aromatic herbs, for at that moment 'the soul and the spirit are separated and sad until the smell comes and unties them and makes glad.'"[42] It is hard to separate from one's gifted additional soul, hard to separate from the majesty of King and Queen (God and his Sh'chinah) and our participation in their nuptials, our foretaste of paradise. Honoring Shabbat, even in ancient times was done with myrtle, as if the Sabbath were a bride, and we are honoring the wedding day on high. How easy it was for later seeing the Sh'chinah as Bride and Queen, and even as Sabbath itself. It is also easy to hear the echoes of honoring the goddess of yore as Queen of Heaven with burning incense and participating in her nuptials – though in the case of Shabbat those nuptials are most certainly not with a son/lover.

Yet another connection with the love goddess is the myrtle itself for the myrtle is symbolic of love and therefore was connected to marriage. In ancient times the groom would carry sprigs of myrtle and wear a garland of myrtle, the bride would be under a canopy of myrtle, a blessing was said over the myrtle. In Hebrew the word for myrtle is Hadassah, the

[41] Urbach, Ephraim E., *The Sages*, chap. I.

[42] Abraham Joshua Heschel, quoting from the Zohar III in *The Sabbath; Its Meaning For Modern Man*, chap. IV, The Noonday Press, 1951.

original name of Queen Esther.[43] The Book of Esther has been interpreted by some as being the Hebrew version – tidied up with moral and ethical meaning – of the springtime love orgies of Ishtar. (Esther as Ishtar and Mordechai as Marduk).[44] The celebration of Purim in remembrance of the Book of Esther is a springtime holiday reminiscent of such abandon, when one is supposed to get drunk, dress up in costumed disguise, and have a wildly good time.[45] In Greek mythology the myrtle is the special plant of the love goddess, Aphrodite.

Ecstasy and love, the feminine principles, are relayed through the Sh'chinah. Among the Hassidim it was claimed that worshipful prayer was made best through song and dance, and this was claimed as the path for everyone, not just the initiates to Kabbalah. These modes of song and dance, of reverence to what we call the feminine principle holds true among the Hassidim to this day, despite those behaviors which so many of us see as rigidly codified, and as a denigration of women in the strict separation of masculine and feminine. (It should be added that this same reasoning could be used to protest against the repression of the masculine, but as far as I know that is yet to come, though the need for it is clear.)

[43] For all of these considerations of Sabbath as marriage, and use of myrtle, see Heschel.

[44] In a most interesting lecture (given at the Dept. of Judaic and Near Eastern Studies at the University of Massachusetts) by Professor Chaim Cohen of the Be'er Sheva University of the Negev, he expounded on his discovery of irrefutable evidence, both historical and philological, that Queen Esther's reign was indeed an actual historical fact. Such historical fact however does not dislodge the truth of a symbolic understanding which adhered to it – when we consciously grant each truth its own arena (cf. beginning of our text, "History & Myth"). In the Kabbalah choosing between truths was separating God from His totality, referred to as "cutting the shoots," making one side only the object of veneration (see my text on the s'fira tree) and considered the worst sin.

[45] The celebration of Mardi Gras is the Christian variation, coming at the same time … before and leading into Easter, as Purim is before and leading into Pesach.

According to Scholem (in contradistinction to what I just wrote in the previous page) the Hassidim did not emphasize the Sh'chinah as feminine. He believes this was a reaction to the devastations caused by the "false messiah," Shabbtai Zvi, who used the sexual symbolism of the Zohar grossly.[46]

The intensity and reverence for the Sh'chinah and her reflection in women lost vitality, as mysticism and orthodoxy stood in competition with the *Haskalah* (Enlightenment) burgeoning in that same period in Europe. New ways of worshipping, far more rational and in tune with "modernity," became prevalent. What was gained in modern enlightenment was lost (to my mind) in spirit. Still, the feminine quality of the Sabbath remains and every Friday evening, in many observant Jewish homes, songs are sung to welcome in the Sabbath Bride and the angels of peace. Candles are lit, challah is baked, dinner is a feast, and singing is done before and after the meal. In my childhood home the singing, and sometimes dancing, lasted well into the night. At Havdallah when the braided candle is lit (indicating the intertwining and distinction of holy and profane) it is still the practice to burn incense or smell myrtle (or some other sweet herb) – to separate the two worlds (holy and profane) which have become one, to give permission to the angels below (of Metatron) to rule the world and its affairs, and accompany the Sh'chinah back to her domain.

The mixture of holy and profane in Judaism is a beautiful blend, not a contamination. The evening times, as in most religions, are magical ... when both realms are mixed ... and in fact the root of the word 'erev' (evening) means 'mixture.' Interplay is essential as we'll see in the next section. At the beginning of Shabbat in declaring, "You shall call the Sabbath (the Sh'chinah) as a guest into your home ..." there is the

---

[46] Gershom Scholem, "Shekhinah," *On The Mystical Shape of the Godhead*, Schocken Books, New York, 1991. For a different interpretation cf. Moshe Idel, *Kabbalah; New Perspectives*, Yale University, 1988

added dictum, "You shall call while it is still day" ... in order
to add a little of the secular to the holy, to honor the Sh'chinah
who is represented by the Sabbath eve. [47]

Today New Moon ceremonies and Women's Sabbaths are
increasingly popular within Judaism – as is goddess consciousness with her ceremonies increasingly popular, arching over all
dogmas. This is happening amongst women who did not
know of the centrality of the Sh'chinah, so well hidden was she
by "enlightenment" and by assimilation. This was particularly
so in Germany, the British Empire and America. Without
throwing away the great gifts of the Enlightenment we are
once again receiving an enlightening that was forever associated with the Sh'chinah, the diffused and radiating light of the
moon.

The prevailing erotic qualities associated with the pagan
love goddess are to this day observed in the Sabbath, albeit
between husband and wife, not communal orgies. Shabbat is
the time for making love. In fact it is a dictum to do so. At any
time, but especially in honor of Shabbat, a husband and wife
making love helps God and his Sh'chinah come together in
lovemaking – and it is in lovemaking that the health and
abundance of the world is continued. A very primitive – and
a very modern – idea.

Sabbath as the time of union of masculine and feminine
principles is spoken of since Talmudic times but the sexes are
reversed, back and forth, showing to my mind, not being
stuck as to who bears the "feminine" and who bears the
"masculine," since both are contained within God. In the
Midrash (*Bereshith Rabba,* par. 11, section 8), "The Sabbath
complains to God: To all the days you gave a partner, only I
have none. 'Then God said to him: the community of Israel
will be your partner.'" ... "The syzygy of the masculine and
feminine is a precondition of the existence of all the worlds."[48]

---

[47] Tishby, chap. "The Sabbath Meals."
[48] Gershom Scholem, *Origins of the Kabbalah,* JPS, Princeton Univ., 1987

Sometimes the Bride is the Sabbath and sometimes the Bride is Israel, while in Kabbalah it is the Sh'chinah who is the Sabbath itself. From a kabbalistic work, *Tikkune Zohar* (1558), interpreting Isaiah 58:13, "If you refrain from trampling the sabbath ... If you call the sabbath 'delight'..." we read, "He who diminishes the delight of the Sabbath, it is as if he robbed the Sh'chinah, for the Sabbath is God's only daughter." The union of lovers in Shabbat reflects the union of lovers in the Book of Ruth, according to Rabbi David Abudraham who lived at Seville, Spain about 1340: "Because the Sabbath and the Community of Israel are the Bride and God is the Groom, we pray: Grant us that we may be like Thy bride, and Thy bride may find tranquillity in Thee, as it is said in *Ruth Rabba*, a woman finds nowhere tranquillity as in her husband."

The quote I used as a dedication to my father at the beginning of this essay – "Remember and Observe" (or "Keep") – is frequently used as representative of the whole meaning of Torah. It refers to the Sabbath, and to its qualities of masculine and feminine union. It is quoting from these portions of Torah: Exodus 20:8, "Remember the sabbath day ..." and Deuteronomy 5:12: "Keep the sabbath day ...." In his work "Origins" where Scholem wrote on the book *Bahir* (the first compilation of Kabbalah in the 12th century) he writes,

> "The two verbs *zakhor* and *shamor*, occurring in the two versions of the Decalogue respectively, at the opening of the commandment enjoining the sanctification of the Sabbath – literally 'mention' or remember, that is actively, and 'keep,' that is passively – are related ... to the masculine and the feminine as principles of the celestial or divine world. The double meaning of *zakhor* – which in Hebrew can signify 'remember' as well as 'masculine' – naturally plays a role in the author's association of ideas. ... the idea that 'keep' refers to the feminine is already found, in an entirely differently context, in *Midrash Tanhuma*."

Referring to the same passage, but this time from the Zohar, Isaiah Tishby writes (quoting from Rabbi Ezra of Gerona's Commentary to the Song of Songs), "And it is well-known that 'Remember' and 'Observe' represent two of the attributes of the Holy One, blessed be He." Also, "keep," *shamor,* can be translated as "guard" and therefore is used as "protection" in referring to the Sh'chinah as well as the doorway on which is affixed the *mezzuzah* which protects the inhabitants within – and which contains the two scriptural passages referring to the unification of Tiferet with the Sh'chinah ... who is the "protector," being the doorway between the upper and lower worlds, protecting form encroachment of the *sitra achra.*

It is in Kabbalah that the feminine and masculine are specified as "attributes" of God, whereas in the prophets, the Bride refers to Israel and in the Talmud the Bride refers to the Sabbath. There are no contradictions here if we hold to the importance of the meaning: it is loving union between masculine and feminine that symbolizes the Torah – and which are heightened on Shabbat.

I believe that the prophets' cries in the Bible played their part in bringing in a new feminine consciousness by decrying the old; while those primal qualities which cannot die, endured in new form specific to the people of Israel, as is told in our text. Ruth, as the new feminine coming from the old pagan religion, follows Naomi into her religion ("... your God shall be my God ..."), and both are transformed in the process. Love-making, fertility, song and well-being, remain central. The threshing floor is still the place where union and love takes place. Accordingly, though the Sh'chinah is Jewish in concept, the general characteristics of pagan goddess remain: Queen and Consort, Mother to the People – just as Ashera was Queen of Heaven and nursing Mother.

And yet – why is it that despite the great power of the feminine, history shows us ever and again – at least in these past three thousand years – the feminine partner in this union being apparently subdued by the masculine? Why? Just because she is powerful?[49] Is it only out of fear of the feminine that women are restrained by show of force? That seems far too flat an explanation, even if partially true. Perhaps it is due to the feminine being repressed within men, which then causes their secret envy, turned frustration, to come out on women? Or is it due to the fear of the irrational (moony) side of life for a mankind so hungry to bring rational order into the universe? I wonder and I have ideas, but all the ideas fall short for they are explanations of the whole by the part. In truth I have to declare "I don't know," and hope that continued wondering will show the way to understanding.

What we all do know, only too well, is the shadow side of the patriarchy,[50] therefore I would like to give emphasis to the word I used, "apparently." Appearances, outer behaviors, are interpreted differently in different ages and cultures. What may be a put-down for some is a "special place" for another. It will be an honor to others and to ourselves if we remember this. Nonetheless I share in the general opinion that the feminine in fact has been painfully restricted, painfully scorned ... and that this has hurt men as well as women. It has hurt our culture, and the pain gives birth to more restrictions, more pain.

Another "apparently" has to do with our conception of woman as moonlight rather than sunlight. Is it not in the nature of the feminine not to shine too forcefully? I definitely do not mean subservience. Nor do I mean that this feminine quality belongs or ought to belong to women alone, let alone all women. There have always been women, as well as goddesses, who fairly reek with brightness and power. An

---

[49] Even in the Kabbalah which shows the equality in value of masculine and feminine – since in fact they are One – the feminine is still shown as powerful and often fearful, whereas I don't read of the masculine as fearful. The feminine is equated with 'deeds' and the masculine with 'words' ... the feminine is the side that does magic ... the feminine in fact is on the left which is associated with evil. There is here a strange paradox (or not so strange) of love, respect and fear.

[50] I am not denying there is a great shadow side of the matriarchy.

attribute that holds men in thrall ... admired by some and found to be utterly fearsome to others – and perhaps as I said above, one of the reasons for enchaining women. To "keep us in our place." There remains however that moon quality which we should not relinquish: the quiet nurturing and subtle influencing that happens far better in the dark than in the bright sun of day. The metaphor of gestation. The truly quiet quality (not repression) belongs to the feminine realm and many women carry it so gracefully – as well those men who are intuitive mediators of the moon realm.

I try to make distinctions, in my daily life as well as theory, between this quiet hidden power and the diminution that comes from learned obedience to outer dictated behaviors.

I cherish the hope that this time around the approaching new union of masculine and feminine as loving and equal partners, each in its own mode, will be a lasting one. At the same time we all know that without conflict and quarrels there is no development. The trick is in knowing how not to cause an irreparable split. So far (in the long view of history) the Great Father and Great Mother have continually kissed and made up, wreaking havoc and creativity along the way.

Hieros Gamos

The archetypal reality expressed in the ancient myths of the divine marriage, the mystical union (*unio mystico)*, is a union of god and goddess, of heaven and earth, from which all fruits of creation emerge. Then, as we're told in another myth, along comes a fellow named Abram, going against his father's ways, breaking up his works, and hearing a disembodied voice of pure spirit as the Creator and Ruler of the universe! What a shock.[51] As I have been stating, the idea born in the early

[51] The period of this new religion is estimated by historians to be about 2,000 B.C.E.

Hebrew religion of a totally spiritual God – creating without having been created, without a mother and without a wife – was a shattering idea, the depths of which most of us still fail to grasp, even as we still shake from its aftershocks. It caused a cataclysmic split in the divine union of masculine and feminine which ran quite deep, as the Book of Ruth testifies. As the Book of Ruth also testifies, the split was not to last (though we are not promised that it won't return in spirals of disharmony and harmony). The idea of the mystical marriage returned into Judaism subtly as the idea of Israel being chosen to be the bride of God.[52] One sees this implied in Exodus, but it comes out in bold articulation with the prophets. There are numerous places in the Bible where God refers to Israel as bride. Our text gives us one such example when it discusses the scene on the threshing floor between Boaz and Ruth – and the symbolic meaning of Ruth's being covered by Boaz' robe. Ezekiel 16:8 is quoted:

> *I passed by you and saw that your time for love had arrived.*
> *So I spread my wing over you and covered your nakedness,*
> *And I entered into a covenant with you by oath – declares*
> *The Lord God – thus you became Mine.*

And in Isaiah 62:4-5:

> *… you shall be called "I delight in her,"*
> *And your land "Espoused." …*
> *And as the bridegroom rejoices over his bride,*
> *So will your God rejoice over you.*

In a most interesting paper with the awkward but descriptive title, "The Image of the Marriage Between God and Israel as it Occurs in the Prophets of the Old Testament, Especially Ezekiel 16" (1950), Rivkah Schärf Kluger wrote on this image of marriage; what it revealed and what it demanded.[53] She speaks of the transformation that took place in the prophet

---

[52] R. Schärf Kluger, "The Idea of The Chosen People," *Psyche in Scripture* (Inner City Books, 1995)

Hosea. She sees in Hosea's railings against the people of Israel
– in his anger at their being an unfaithful wife to God –
Hosea's *own* inability to resolve his personal inner conflict
between nature and spirit. This was a problem constellated by
the new religion which had made distinctions between the
two. In her article R. Schärf Kluger writes:

> "Looked at from the psychological point of view, the emergence
> of the marriage image means a more intimate and inward
> approach of the people toward the spiritual God, Yachveh; an
> increasing receptivity toward the spiritual principle. But before
> advancing further in this direction the people had first to *become*
> *aware of their own nature and in this phase of development they*
> *remained stuck. That was their unfaithfulness.* (italics mine) Only
> a few progressed further: the prophets. They … were the sensitive
> exponents of this struggle. They were able to stand up to this
> inner conflict. They entered into the marriage and were faithful
> to it. The sign of this is that God speaks to them.
> "… The underlying (problem) of Hosea's marriage seems to me
> to be the fact that he was himself still caught in his inner conflict.
> Marriage with a faithless wife indicates a psychological marriage
> with his own unconscious faithless soul. Through the pain he
> suffers on account of his wife's unfaithfulness he experiences, in
> projected form, his own unfaithfulness. He (later) realizes God's
> faithfulness in his own body and his own soul, and through this
> experience he himself receives the psychic feminine attitude in
> his marriage with God."

To express this realization she quotes the beginning of the
passage of Hosea 2:16, which passage I include in its entirety,
for it also appears in our text (chap. 3:5, p. 75):

> *Assuredly,*
> *I will welcome her*
> *And bring her into the wilderness*
> *And speak to her tenderly.*

[53] Taken here from a taped informal reading, in honor of R. Schärf Kluger's 70th
birthday, but appearing in *Spring*, New York, 1950.

I will give her her vineyards from there,
And the Valley of Achor as a plowland of hope.
There she shall respond as in the days of her youth,
When she came up from the land of Egypt.
And in that day
– declares the Lord –
You will call Me Ishi (my husband)
And no more will you call Me Ba'ali (my Lord).

I include all of this to show how our meeting and welcoming of the goddess these days points not only to our openhearted acceptance, but is a great call to consciously and conscientiously recognize within ourselves our own natures. This new consciousness of a feminine function still needs attentive discipline in order for us to be good disciples, which term I use in its positive sense of being a dedicated student. Where are we in *our* "inner conflicts"? How much of our own lack do we project onto the god/goddess images when we receive either too hungrily or too critically? too readily, without discrimination? as when we think of the Goddess as equaling Good – confusing "necessity" with "goodness"; or when we pose in combat Goddess against God, thereby insisting on the split that nature and spirit are so wanting to heal.

We have come sufficiently of age to know that "Goddess is Great" means only that: Abundant. Nowadays we may modify the cry of the prophets to "Careful!" rather than "Don't!"

Accepted or not the ancient goddesses have continued to live in our psyches, even in their pre-historic forms, connecting us ever and again with the power of the feminine; not necessarily 'good' or 'bad,' but Sheer Existence – sometimes exhibiting one quality, sometimes another. It bodes well to welcome wisely such goddess power for she visits us in dreams where she brings to light those places where we have remained in the dark. She apparently wants us to help her manifest well.

A modern middle-aged woman announced one day,
"Enough of this high priestess shit! I have to get back to my
very own womanhood." She was in the throes of mourning
the death of her father, and finally worn down in a torment
that came from five months of following his request to lead his
soul after death to the "other side." The night after her
exclamation came the following dream:

> *I am walking on city streets at the head of a procession of young,*
> *somber, uniform men in black. I am looking for a new place to work.*
> *Without warning I am lifted into space, slowly ascending. I am*
> *tremendously frightened, but very quiet. I rise further and further*
> *knowing that I am going "North" to the outer unknown reaches of*
> *the universe ... and that I must. I feel my body organs moving about*
> *(re-organizing!) inside of me. I continue slowly to rise far, far above*
> *the earth. Awful fear continues to fill me. Suddenly I see looming*
> *before and above me, at a tremendous height of uncountable*
> *measure, the Great Woman. She looks just like the Venus of Laussel.*
> *She stands in space between the continents of Africa and Asia. All*
> *three are of the same tremendous size, all are suspended in space. I*
> *know with a great sense of glory and revelation that this is the real*
> *world, of which our little world below is a reflection. I am being*
> *faced with utter Reality. The way it is. Wondrous and awe-full. The*
> *Great Woman announces in a voice that rings through everywhere,*
> *"I AM AFRICA. I AM ASIA." I know I have heard the Truth and*
> *that I will be changed forever. I descend slowly back through space*
> *and am once again on the city streets, continuing the journey,*
> *searching for a place to work. I am changed but it cannot be seen*
> *outwardly.*

The Venus of Laussel is a Paleolithic carving in *bas relief*
dating to about 20 000–30 000 B.C.E. She holds up a horn or
a crescent moon in her hand and she stands at the entrance to
a cave in Les Eyzies, France. The dreamer associated her with
rituals of initiation which entailed facing the forces of death
within the cave, and rebirth if one got through it. This was the
true image of what she had been pressed to do, the high
priestess who led souls in *rites de passage*.

In this dream the Great Woman came as the reality of the world, its source and its meaning; it's creation. Yet it was not in competition with God the Father that she appeared. She just "was" – absolute Being – and her appearance to the dreamer was a reminder of Her, and her, reality. An ancient, primal womanhood, a Creator Goddess, assuring the woman that she needn't be contaminated with high priestess shit, any more than she need be identified as daughter-to-the-father in obedience to his dictates to lead his soul – nor did she have to be tormented by fulfilling those talents – but she did have to know the *source and goal* of her obedience and actions. She had also to be assured that her own work would be continued in the everyday life, looking for her own place to work, in the full knowledge that she had a reflection above, and was reflected back, by The Great Woman, the Creator of all. In a word, the dream responded to her cry, "I have to get back to my own womanhood," differentiating (making conscious) the roles of goddess and woman.

I return then to my idea that the meaning and intent of the prophets' passions spoke not only against the pagan sexual practices but spoke rather to the backsliding submission to an *unconscious* feminine force, an adoration of the *undifferentiated* feminine – the pagan feminine as ambivalent; birth and devouring, loving and castrating (as referred to in our text) rather than pointing to a greater consciousness vis-à-vis the smaller, as we saw in the dream above.

Africa and Asia are our ancestral homes, the birthplaces of the Great Goddesses that we do find alluring, and whose varied qualities we are rediscovering in both their negative and positive aspects. Once again our century has come to appreciate the feminine forms of lust and liveliness that give birth to a creative life bound not only by moralisms. Spontaneity is being valued ... at least in theory. Intuition is increasingly being given as much verity as intellect, empathy as much value as control. Once again we see her allure as gift and not as threat. In honor to our feminine breadth and compassion, we should see this ability to accept goddess-power as due (historically if not personally) to our having passed through a time of the power of the masculine – which now backs us up. Which is to say, that self-same masculine spirit that can bind us restrictively, may also be sufficiently integrated to uphold us – not to get swept away in subjective subjugation.

No doubt the masculine spirit was not yet integrated in the early days of the Bible therefore the allure was still overly prevalent ... just as these days she can be to those who remain too naïve, too adoring. One pervasive illustration of this "backsliding" today would be the "oh-wow" adoration of the magnitude of the unconscious, described in our text as submission to the goddess (sometimes via drugs but not necessarily), which devalues the masculine attributes of action, will and individual choice (consciousness), castrating oneself in honor of the moon, the mother-lover Cybele, as did her priests in Asia Minor. There is no transformation in this adoration, just a 'round-and-'round rut of repetition. The value of cyclical nature ruled by the feminine moon with her diffused poetic light, is beautiful indeed, but creative only when experienced in relation to the clear outlines and warmth of the sunlight. Making choices of preference between the two, putting them in opposite camps, is either a sad attempt to retrieve the goddess, or an equally sad defense against her real epiphany. Sad, for in such one-sided ways we are going against the very nature of the goddess as brooding, as inclusive. The first attempt is infantile wish-fulfillment, the second is the senex defense we know too well as "Puritanical" moralities. I far prefer to see the moon and sun aspects, the feminine and masculine, as the Kabbalists do when they see love-making as the unity of God – where the Sh'chinah is described as the "throne" of Tiferet, and Tiferet making love with his Sh'chinah, is expressed as, "Tiferet sitting on his throne."

Sun and Moon

Obviously the competition between sun and moon has been going on for some time. Just listen to some of the *midrashim* that show this rivalry.[54]

One story: On the fourth day God created the sun and the moon. At first the sun and moon were equal in size and brightness. The moon, in true feminine fashion, had wily ways and asked very clever but insinuating questions of God, beginning with His creation of the world, to which she received wise answers, and to which she fool-heartedly continued rhetorically questioning until reaching her final point, made by using God's reasoning of 'lesser and greater,' "... you have created the sun and the moon, and it is becoming that one of them should be greater than the other." God responded to the moon, "I know well you would have me make you greater than the sun. As a punishment I decree that you may keep but one-sixtieth of your light!" The moon replied, "Shall I be punished so severely for having spoken a single word?" and God relented, "In the future world I will restore your light so that it may again be as the light of the sun." Not satisfied the moon continued, "O Lord, the light of the sun, how great will it be in that day?" God's wrath was kindled, "What? You still plot against the sun?! As you live, in the world to come his light shall be sevenfold the light he now sheds."

A similar story: The sun and moon were created as equal, one ruling the night, the other day. They began to quarrel as to who was better and because of this jealousy between them God decided to punish one of them. He chose the moon to be diminished since the moon had intruded into the sphere of the sun (as when the moon is seen in the sky during daytime).

In a turnabout of the above story God repents and lessens his punishment of the moon by allowing it to be in the realm

---

[54] Louis Ginzberg, *The Legends of the Jews*, Volumes I and V. (Jewish Publication Society, 1968)

of the sun, whereas the sun cannot be in the realm of the moon.

Another story: When God punished the envious moon by diminishing her light and her splendor, she fell – and tiny threads were loosed from her body. These are the stars.

Yet another story, an amazing one: The sacrifice of atonement, the he-goat offered on the new moon, is God's sin-offering, His acknowledgment that He dealt too severely with the moon! He also compensated the moon for its reduction in size by having it become the symbol of Israel and the pious, whereas the sun represented Essau and the ungodly.

In the myth's original form the sun and the moon are endowed with wisdom and passion, just as is man.

One can see in these stories how attitudes toward sun and moon consciousness were not fixed, as also their gender is not central. Still, one tends to think of the moon as feminine, at least in the west and often in Judaism where the moon is Rachel and/or the Sh'chinah, though sometimes it is Isaac who carries the meaning of moon, as also is Perez. Not all of the stories of sun and moon have the two in conflict. We have in the Zohar Ruth, in elucidating proverbs 4:18, "She [Rachel] is called 'the moon' which traverses the entire night to give them light until 'complete day,' which is Jacob." This is in accordance with (among other commentaries) Genesis Rabbah 2:3, which says the light created by God on the first day is Jacob.

The blessing of the new moon belongs very much to the woman's ritual and there were various ways of participating in this over the ages. Always it was a time of rejoicing with music and prayers of thanksgiving – thanksgiving for renewal in nature as well as of Israel's renewal and redemption.[55] (The Sh'chinah, being closest to earth, is moon, is nature, is the Knesset Israel, and is Israel.) The feminine aspect is also emphasized in the Talmud which says, "Whoever pronounces

---

[55] Cf. Encyclopedia Judaica under "Moon."

the benediction over the new moon in its due time welcomes, as it were, the presence of the Shekhinah," and, as far back as the Second Temple the blessings of the new moon were celebrated with dancing and rejoicing.

My excursion into sun and moon stories – aside from indulging in the sheer enjoyment of them – is in order for us to see by the light of the same tradition as exists in our Ruth and Naomi story, aspects of sun and moon consciousness reflecting unendingly our swings between, and unions of, opposite modes which are usually envisioned as masculine and feminine. In most cultures the moon as light of the night belongs to the realm of the non-rational, the receptive, the moody, the ecstatic, carrying the attribute of emotion ... those qualities which have been associated with the feminine.

Our culture has had need to return to moon-intoxication in its winding path of welcoming back the feminine, so perhaps I shouldn't be too scolding of our anxiously scooping up the beams. My caution comes from having witnessed the destruction this pendulum swing has brought about. One one-sidedness certainly can't cure another, since it is one-sidedness itself which is the culprit ... and yet, this is also to be expected. What is new bursts in exuberantly, without discipline, without discrimination. All the more reason to be astonished at the graceful acknowledgment of "the new" in the Book of Ruth.

The allure of the moon (Ruth) needs the reverential action of love-making if consciousness is to come into being. This is the part that Boaz plays in fulfilling and redeeming not only Ruth but Naomi, and thereby himself, and ultimately through their son's descendant, all of humanity. This love story between sun and moon consciousness is (to use moon terms) increasingly inspiring.

All of which brings to mind a dream of about 20 years ago, but a dream which is more in the mode of the prophets' urgency than is my lenient and fair acceptance of just a few lines ago. This is a dream of the potential arising from the union of masculine and feminine, seen in a nighttime vision, demanding utmost daytime consciousness:

> *It is a dark night and I am standing alone on the streets of Jerusalem. The air is soft and clear, and as usual on those velvet nights, the stars are close. Suddenly they being to move rapidly about. Half of the stars become intensely red and the other half bright white. These colors represent masculine and feminine (though which is which is neither clear nor important) and their moving in graceful swirls of patterns, in and out of one another and round about, is their love-making. It is of tremendous import that I pay close attention. We all must pay close attention.*
> *This numinous happening is a proclamation for everyone to view. The proclamation is about nothing less than an immanent new aeon whose manifestation is dependent upon us human beings. By our proper viewing we will actively participate in the outcome – by paying strict attention we will enable the love-making to manifest itself for the good – for a manifestation is sure to take place one way or another. If we devotedly pay attention this coupling will manifest as Creation and Redemption – if we don't pay attention it means total Destruction. This is a portent regarding all existence.*
> *I am filled with the urgency of this great happening and its demand upon us. I call out in the streets, "Look! Everyone look!!" But no one pays attention. I go here and there calling in all directions, "Look!" Finally a young man of the hippie type notices the stars I am pointing to. He looks up, smiles, and in ga-ga appreciation drawls, "Oh wow." "No!" I shout at him, "It is not 'oh wow'; it is important, it is urgent!" and I continue to call for people to look, and the stars continue to swirl in magnificent patterns, filling the sky. The time is now.*

*
* *

Let's return to the beginning of our chapter, to Naomi in Moab, during another time in history when the wished for birth of redemption arising from the *hieros gamos* is promising to transpire; a redemption arising from the union of masculine and feminine. Here is Naomi, a woman already re-formed by the spirit of the masculine Yachveh, now re-newing her soul by sitting in the lap of the feminine Ashtarot.

I believe it is not true to the character of Naomi to have participated in the goddesses' rituals for there is too much in her ... as well as in the meaning of the story ... that has her firmly a daughter of Yachveh. If this were not the case then she would not at all be the appropriate receiver of the *new* feminine. She would simply be repeating the past and back-sliding into pagan idolatry.[56] She would have remained in Moab. Hers is a story of change from within, not conversion to without. A true synthesis. Therefore my question is answered: Whether or not Naomi's compassion allowed her daughters-in-law their ancestral ways, or whether or not they invited her participation in ritual, is irrelevant. It is surely the *atmosphere* of Moab, saturated as it were with the love goddess – and the fact of Naomi's *being* in it – that had its effect. And it is Naomi – whose ancestry has already experienced and integrated the excruciating demands of the new masculine, spiritual religion – who now is able to invite and expedite the goddess of old into *her* own transformation, redeeming what was lacking in both. A two-way process.

I am thinking of Rachel stealing her father's *teraphim,* as we are reminded in our text. Rachel didn't make it to Bethlehem, she died on the way.[57] Naomi, also on the way to Bethlehem, undergoes a major transformation, and this due to the same ingredient: *teraphim,* household idols. But now Naomi is reversing the process. She is bringing back, not the *teraphim* per se, but something of the *quality* they portrayed, the erotic fullness of the love goddess. Naomi does not cling to the past as did Rachel, but has gleaned from it what Rachel, in her day,

[56] This is a story of transformation and individuation. Individuation is inclusive, not throwing out the past's "errors" but integrating all – the goal being totality. The principle is teleological, the mode dialectical, the process difficult.

[57] Not as a punishment but as symbolic of the times – and for the "divine purpose" of being intermediary between humanity and God ... as Mother of all her peoples she intercedes with God on their behalf.

had to forcibly discard. And like Rachel she becomes the mother for her people.

How hard it is to go to the Other Side in order to regain (or rescue, or glean – or to kill, as in the myths of heroism) what is necessary without falling under its spell; without succumbing to it or identifying with The Other. Sometimes such submission to The Other is a necessary step before coming out the other end and into a new reality. We are not told if Naomi went through such a phase; apparently it is sufficient to see her as enduring. We learn from Naomi, who has certainly gained a new consciousness in Moab, that it is enough to truly *be* in the milieu ... to be touched by it ... and to be kind to it.

I find this new consciousness evident in the phrase, "Naomi heard that God had taken note of His people." Our text uses that phrase to describe how the deaths of the two sons (the product of the 'old' masculine consciousness) allowed the space for the new attitude to step in. I am adding to this the change that occurred within Naomi herself, by sitting in those surroundings that rang true to her woman nature. The change in the *sit*uation of the old feminine caused God to "take note."

Some translations have it that God "remembered" his people. That's the translation I read as a child and I wondered what kind of a God would forget. Taking note indicates more of a reciprocity to my mind. "I'm watching, but what are *you* doing? I'm getting bored stiff with your stiff-neckedness. Aha! You bend? Oh yes, my lost dove. I see you now." Something like that.

CHAPTER 6

Call Me Mara
"From Sweet to Bitter, from Bitter to Sweet"

After meeting the goddess, how is she received? Naomi, for all of her patience and endurance, does not encourage her entry; at least not that we can tell by her initial reception of Ruth. "Too soon! Too soon!" something in her conservative nature may have been saying. "Call me Mara," Naomi says to the women of Bethlehem when they are all in a turmoil over her return and the change they see in her. Naomi does not recognize at first the inner change that has occurred, a change made manifest by Ruth's clinging to her – and even then noticed only by God and us the readers ... and according to our text, by the women of Bethlehem – but not by Naomi. What is dramatically evident to her is her loss; so devastating that she is not seeing clearly.

This makes sense, sounds familiar, doesn't it? At any time the loss of a husband and especially the loss of one's children (that creature creation of mine to whom I gave life, to whom I am responsible and with whom I am attached as to nothing else, having been born from my body and my soul) is a devastating event beyond words. Imagine how much more so in a time when a woman's identity was totally bound up with being wife and mother.

Wait! How dare I take this cultivated high ground! I remember a time when I was that primitive woman. I was sitting on the floor of my analyst's office, becoming increasingly frustrated at his cool clear surety that I get on with my individuation (in this instance pictured as pursuing my profession); insisting on this at a time I was feeling so in despair, so desperately wanting another child and having heard I couldn't have one. "You don't understand," I wailed at him, "I *am* two breasts and a uterus!" And this I said with full conviction. I, a modern woman.

I know that we retain somewhere our non-enlightened primal femininity, what our text calls the "natural woman," even if not in this mother-oriented way. What a burden of consciousness that places upon us. How to be both; primal being and enlightened person all at once. More specific to our story: how to find our own way, our continuing new way, when all seems taken away. How to continue life in the face of death's stealing our love, our loved ones, our identity.

Anyone reading this must remember a time when a marriage broke down, or up, or a love affair ended, or a beloved died. That feeling of the lights going out, no colors in the world and life loosing meaning. I have known that and certainly have witnessed the experience in others. I have seen women who have fallen into bitterness and misery over the loss of a husband or lover or child ... by whatever means. They readily said, "Call me Mara" and saw no end to it. It did no good to remind them that this was not the totality of their meaning in life ... especially if during the time it was. No good whatsoever to propound theories and promises, or talk of fatefulness.

Time and patience and sitting *in* it proves to be the best response, the groundwork for allowing the unconscious to "take note." Giving Time his due, granting to Patience her rhythm, sitting in the quiet space within. What happens in that response is that eventually a whole new identity is discovered. Not by will or choice – except by the will to choose patience. Women during pregnancy have patience because there is no other way. We passively watch ourselves become another shape, emotionally as well as physically, and cannot do otherwise *if* we want to guard well the new life. If the metaphor of pregnancy doesn't do it for you, find another time when you were not able, by any means, to go about your habitual life. A time of illness, paralysis, amputation, or as in our story, a time of forced removal from home, which appears to bring nothing but death.

Unlike the way most of us were raised in the western world, bereavement is not always a time for "coping," for gathering one's strength to forge ahead, or of fighting to change the situation. Besides, in such cases the enemy we choose to fight is usually not the right one. These are not the times for that sun-heroic consciousness. In our story we are reminded of Naomi's way being the woman's way. Bearing, enduring and waiting ... for the right time.

Shortly after writing this a friend just happened to bring my attention to the poem "East Coker" by T.S. Eliot:

> *"I said to my soul, be still, and*
> *wait without hope,*
> *For hope would be hope for the wrong thing: Wait*
> *Without*
> *Love*
> *For love would be love of the wrong thing; There is yet*
> *Faith*
> *But the faith and the love and the hope are all in the*
> *waiting."*

Being brought to a standstill requires standing still. In such terrible times patience not achieved leaves us in the dismal abyss of frustration, depression, or a bitter cynicism that calls itself reality. Oh to learn this patience in our times of deathly despair! Patience, *not* optimism! An optimistic outlook, too early in the process, could well undercut the necessary boiling in hell that causes transformation. But patience to bear it, *while* truthfully declaring our current being as bitter – that's the true talent. Naomi states things as they are but does not wallow in self pity. Realizing that there is nothing to do, giving up on forcing fate, is where the "healing dreams" come in.

A woman during a severe depression, and after realizing there was nowhere to go and nothing to be done, dreams:

> *I am walking barefoot in a bare and dry landscape of thorns. Nothing to be seen anywhere but endless flat earth of grey-brown thorns. My feet are being cut, everything hurts. I keep walking, one foot in front of the other, staring at my bruised, hurting feet, walking, walking. After a while I hear a man's voice which comes from everywhere. A serious voice telling me very wise things. I concentrate hard, with all my might, on listening to and understanding these words of wisdom. Little by little, bits of green clover appear among the thorns. They increase. They take the place of the thorns. Soon I am walking entirely on clover. It is cool and moist and soothing. My feet no longer hurt. I look up for the first time in the dream and can see the curve of the earth, extending to the horizon, a vast rounded view of luscious fields of clover.* [58]

When she awoke she felt "alive" for the first time in months, alive and hopeful. Allowing the psyche to give its very own timely answers is what is meant by "process." Such humble attitude even stimulates the response of the psyche.

This unaffected endurance is what Naomi has – without proclamations or conscious concepts of "process" – and this is what causes the change in her that makes God "take note" … perhaps even helps him "remember" His people, His bride.

---

[58] This dream brings to mind the earlier dream of the dancing woman removing a thorn from her foot, but what a difference in the women … and therefore a difference in how the thorn is received. This dream is of a young woman, and in a state where she still is needing protection from the harshness of the thorn side of life which has come to hit her so hard. See how "kind" the unconscious is! to give only that which can be received. This same quality is found in the Sh'chinah.

The S'firot Tree

The Mother in our story has gone from being Naomi to Mara, from Mara to Naomi. It is said of the Sh'chinah that she goes from "sweet to bitter, from bitter to sweet." So that we may gain the large picture of those dynamics which lie within our story, let's take a look again at the s'firot tree (p. 76 of our text) as it was revealed and described through the Zohar and elaborated through the Kabbalah of Isaac Luria.[59]

This "tree" is a schematic representation of the qualities of God as these work dynamically *within* the godhead and as they emanate *from* the godhead into the world – from whose inhabitants God receives, and is effected, in return. This is an ongoing interchange and influence between divine and profane. Just above the s'fira is the *Ein Sof* (lit. "without end," not pictured in our diagram), the Hidden God, the creative nothingness out of which all creation derives. Because the scheme represents the flow of God from his hidden depths to His emanations – as well from infinity into creation, it is called a tree whose roots are above and whose branches are below. The qualities (or forces, or energies) are called s'firot, each one is a s'fira[60].

Within the godhead these s'firot – inasmuch as it is all a living, moving and continually creating God – have relations

---

[59] The following is a gross simplification done not to actually explain the s'firot tree as much as it is to show only the simplest aspects in order to shed light on a kabbalistic meaning, which I've found so apparent, in the Book of Ruth.

[60] The word '*s'fira*' (usually transliterated as sephira) does not mean 'sphere,' as is often misunderstood. These are not different spheres but are 10 distinct and interacting qualities within the Godhead. The word '*s'fira*' may come from the word for 'number' (*s'fira*) for in early Kabbalah they were referred to by number and not name (which came about 400 years later). It may be also be "number" referring to the Decalogue by which statements the world was created, according to Kabbalah. Again, since the word for "number" and "tell" are the same root, it could be the statements by God in His creating the world, "And God said ..." Another idea is that it may come from a word meaning 'sapphire' (*sapir*) referring to their light, radiance.

with one another, they influence one another, they flow. The paths of flow are through the "branches," the "shoots," the "channels," such as we see in the drawing. So – the masculine s'firot (on the right) and feminine s'firot (on the left) each have their own partners, their own mates, and the flow of intercourse between them is the flow of loving union. The s'firot tree is an elaborate system of the sacred marriage, *hieros gamos*, the act of love between god and goddess – in this case all being within the single God who is composed equally of masculine and feminine attributes. The entire s'firot tree is of the holy marriage, the *hieros gamos.*

The lowest s'fira, called Malchut (Kingdom) represents the Sh'chinah and is the gateway between holy and profane (being closest to the world, the kingdom on earth). You can see Malchut in our drawing at the bottom center, opposite the top center, Keter. Keter (Crown) is sometimes called the "hidden thought" of God, and it is the Sh'chinah that brings this into the world, she "completes the thought" it is said. She is also called Atara [diadem] as counterpart to Keter [crown]. – The Sh'chinah is the manifestation, the *realization* of God's will. At the very, center of the s'firotic system, it's central pillar, you see Tiferet (Beauty) and "he" is the partner to the Sh'chinah. She receives all the abundance from above in her union with him as it is channeled through Yesod (Foundation, or, Righteous).

Tiferet is also called the "Mystery of Faith," while the Sh'chinah is called "Faith." One could say that bringing faith into our living reality depends upon our reception of the mystery.

It is the Sh'chinah that receives. She receives all – from both realms. From above she receives all the emanations of the divine, masculine and feminine; from below she receives the prayers, deeds, and attitudes (intentions) of humanity. She is the final vessel and channel for all that comes from above and is the port of entry for all that comes from below. She unites above and below. She receives from both directions and she gives to both directions ... those qualities and energies *as they have come through her.*

The s'firot when in proper loving flow are harmonious and the Sh'chinah receiving the divine abundance via her partner Tiferet, distributes it to the world below. Sometimes the harmony is broken, and then there is an imbalance, a preponderance comes from the left side, Din (Judgment), also known as G'vurah (Power or Strength). When Din is not in flow with her partner Hesed (Love, Loving-kindness) – which is to say, when judgment and power overrule loving kindness – there is an imbalance, both in the upper and in the lower realms. Too much of the Din power flowing into the Sh'chinah causes her to be bitter.

We can see from our diagram how it is that the Sh'chinah is referred to as the "Great sea into which all rivers flow." As sea she collects the fullness of all the rivers and nourishes the world with her water, which water changes from *sweet to bitter and bitter to sweet,* according to whether there is more Din or more Hesed.

The Sh'chinah is not merely a two way clearing house through which all divine qualities and human deeds pass. Being the container she reflects what she contains, but more to the point: being the feminine aspect of God she has definite feminine qualities and (as noted above) is the defender and protector of the people, even to the point of contending with God (God vis-à-vis Himself). She is the mother, the queen, the daughter, the princess, and the lover. She has an erotic quality as well as a mothering one: she is the lover of Tiferet, the Bride of God, and the point of concentration when men are making love to their wives ... over which act she presides. Through her union with Tiferet, who is known as the "perfect reconciliation between the two extremes of Love and Judgment" (Hesed and Din) – and therefore known also as Rehamim (Compassion) – the Sh'chinah receives and metes out what is appropriate.

(Is that not a wonderful description of compassion? – A reconciliation of love and judgment.)

"When she ascends, she ascends like a dove, and when she descends, she descends like an eagle, for she is the consort who is not afraid of any bird in the world – and she descends with food for her young. ... To each one she brings down the food that is suitable for him. ... To some she brings down the food of the Torah, which is food for the soul; and to some she brings down food for the body: to each according to his desire (or 'need')."[61]

The Sh'chinah is most generally thought of in this benevolent aspect, where she is the protector and the nurturing mother – in accordance with humanity's needs. She is described as the Lower Mother, in relation to Binah who is the Upper Mother. You see Binah in the drawing as the first s'fira on the left, the feminine side. She is called Understanding, or, Intelligence and is the partner of the masculine side, Hochma, "Wisdom." This pair is the "father and mother," the remaining seven s'firot having been emanated through their union. Therefore we have two mothers, as we do in the Book of Ruth: Binah and the Malchut, Binah as the Upper Mother birthing the s'firot and Malchut as Lower Mother, bringing all that birthing into the world, i.e., the manifestation of the mothering ... the realization. (All of the attributes and dynamics of the Sh'chinah can readily be seen as in keeping with her main designation as "Presence" and as "Sovereign" of the world.) As mentioned when talking of Anatot, the doubling of the goddess is a psychological truth in religions and we see it in mother/maiden duos such as Demeter/Persephone as well as pairs of opposites such as Christianity's Virgin Mary and Mary Magdalene. The same happens here with Malchut and

---

[61] Tishby, This particular quote is from *The Wisdom of the Zohar; An Anthology of Texts*, Vol. III, p. 1056., Oxford University Press, 1989. Most of my references will be from these three volumes of Tishby's – and from Gershom Scholem's *Origins* and *Kabbalah*, Keter, Jerusalem, 1974

Binah, who also both represent the Sh'chinah, the Upper Sh'chinah and the Lower Sh'chinah.

It is through Binah as mother that all emanation proceeds. Her partner, Hochma (Wisdom) is also called Reshit, "Beginning" and is referred to as the father. The first line of the Torah: *B'reshit bara elohim*, usually read as "In the beginning God created" is interpreted mystically as referring to the first three s'firot in the process of birthing the creation and could be read, "The Beginning (Hesed) created God (Binah)! Binah is also called 'elohim.'" This gives a picture of the combination of forces through which creation took (takes) place. The Creation takes place through the union of the Mother and the Father. Very much the Great Mother.

As noted, there are positive and negative aspects in the Sh'chinah; an ambivalence reminiscent of the Great Goddess. Her sweetness can turn to bitter when there is an imbalance on the side of Din. These bitter times come from the Sh'chinah being cut off from Tiferet, for when the Sh'chinah is filled too much with Din Tiferet *withdraws* from her. Then she is 'like a pregnant woman whose goodness is imprisoned and held back inside of her. She cannot give birth.' Without Tiferet she becomes 'a lonely and abandoned woman.' In such a state she becomes without voice, mute. Psalm 39 is heard as the Sh'chinah's saying, "I was dumb and silent. I held my peace to no avail. My distress grew worse. My heart became hot within me." In the extreme this negative aspect can reach down to the very point of being called *Ilana di Mota,* the Tree of Death. As the Tree of Death she 'rules over the lower world and because everything is below her she consumes and destroys it.' She literally becomes the "devouring mother."

The result of Tiferet withdrawing from the Sh'chinah is that she then falls into the *sitra achra*, the Other Side, and into the clutches of Sama'el, and it is he with whom she unites. Now then, the *sitra achra* is not of the s'firot tree but is as if a mirror image of that realm; paradoxical inasmuch as it is considered totally other and at the same time mirroring and playing its destined and therefore divine part. It has it's own ruler, Sama'el, the king of demons with his consort, Lilit. Although this "falling" of the Sh'chinah is a tragedy for both the upper realm and the world below, there is a divine necessity in it. As noted above when talking of sacrifice (p. 130ff) evil has its place in redemption. The Other Side is the place where the lost value is found.[62]

That split, that "cutting of the shoots" is caused not by an arbitrary happening within the s'firotic system, but by the actions of humanity. When there has been human error or sin, and where there has been too much cleaving to the left side of God (always referring to Din) it causes an imbalance which results in a disruption of the harmonic flow, within God and therefore within the world. This is the greatest evil and the greatest tragedy. One-sidedness. It is in fact the origin of sin. Its story goes like this: The tree in the center of the Garden of Eden is The Tree of Life (Tiferet) and the Tree of Knowledge (the Sh'chinah). Originally they were one tree (though there are somewhat different variations to the story, but the meaning is the same.) Adam was commanded by God to cleave to the Tree of Life. Adam however when he picked the fruit was separating the fruit from the tree and thereby separating the Sh'chinah from Tiferet. This meant he was cleaving to the Sh'chinah alone, in her separation from Tiferet ... thereby causing a split in the divine lovers, a cataclysmic break in the unity of God. The result is that Adam (mankind) is then ruled by the Sh'chinah (we live in an age ruled by Din, an eon of 6,000 years) and is subject to her vacillations from bitter to sweet, sweet to bitter. Worse, when the Sh'chinah is separated from Tiferet she becomes the Tree of Death (mortality came into the world with Adam's sin). The origin of sin is not eating forbidden fruit, it is splitting feminine and masculine by

---

[62] The fall into the *sitra achra* coming with the separation of Tiferet and the Sh'chinah is reminiscent of the descent of Innana into the realm of Erishkagel – both being necessary hells for continuing redemptions.

worshipping (eating from) *one aspect alone*, by making one side alone the object of veneration.[63]

When the Sh'chinah is without Tiferet she is in exile and in mourning. She wears black. With the split between King and Queen there can no longer be the loving flow into the world below. God has become cut off from his Sh'chinah ... the flow of abundance ceases ... the unity of God has been torn and is hurting. No wonder this is the greatest evil.

This should come as no surprise considering that the creation and well being of the world are dependent upon the *hieros gamos*, the *unio mystica* spoken of above. It is just this one-sidedness with which the Book of Ruth opens its story.

*
* *

It should be apparent by now how I would see these dynamics reflected in the story of Ruth, as that story of redemption is expounded in our text. We are told in our text that Ruth, the means of redemption, comes from the other side, the side of the enemy and the side of the despised religion – and in the Zohar Ruth from the *sitra achra,* stated as such. Psychologically, individuation can only take place after entering the feared Other Side, the unconscious. That realm of the unknown, totally other, is where we meet our demons and angels – our worse traits that rule us in a compulsive way, a shadowy way, as well as finding there our lost doves and unknown, yet unborn, gifts. It is also the arena of death ... ego orientation dissolves ... which death may bring rebirth, renewal.

In addition to the above, I view the dynamics of the s'firot tree to be reflected in the condition and the personality of Naomi. Not literally a translation, but effectively and affectively resounding in her and the entire story.[64] I see Naomi's bitterness as being under the influence of the sufferings of the Sh'chinah, in the bitter waters of the Sh'chinah "under whose

---

[63] I like to point out here that Eve is not the guilty party.

wings ..." or, "in whose shadow – or secret – *all* women stand." The consequences of the exile of the Sh'chinah is easily seen in Bethlehem's famine, and the ensuing Tree of Death was certainly active for the men of the family of Elimelech ... and therefore for Naomi who was left alone to mourn them, reflecting the mourning Sh'chinah in black ... without children ... without grandchildren ... with barren daughters-in-law ... with nothing but sterility as her endowment.

After such an experience it will take a long time to sweeten bitterness ... a long time to realize that Binah is effecting her actions; Binah, the ever emanating, Intelligent, Understanding, Mother. An action of devoted love, such as Ruth's, might well be overlooked – just as an inner change might not yet be self apparent. The advent of Boaz helps her remember, helps her to consciously take a hand in fate,,, and it is the person of Boaz (representing Yesod and thereby being the agent) that brings in Tiferet, just as Ruth brings in the Sh'chinah in her loving and fertile aspect.

At the end of my second chapter I wrote, "... God does not speak at all in this story ... at least, not out loud." When I wrote the sentence I had no idea how much I would mean that. I now see that it is not only Ruth as bringing in the Sh'chinah, or Boaz as representative of Yesod (both as stated in our text) ... and it is not just the equation I make with Naomi as Binah as creator (Elohim) herself ... what strikes me now is how much the *entire* story reads as though it were written under the aegis, so to speak, of the Sh'chinah, Upper and Lower. And therefore I return to my original realization, "This is a woman's story!" but this time with more intricacies behind it, "This is the Sh'chinah's story"![65]

---

[64] The Zohar Ruth however does go into highly intricate interpretations which do make direct connections between the s'firot and the sitra achra and the characters of the story.

CHAPTER 7

Receiving Ruth – Returning Orpah

In order to make real the reception of the new feminine consciousness, a conscious choice had to be faced up to. Naomi had to be put on the spot, or rather, the goddess image had to be put on the spot. Here in the crux of the story, on the way to Bethlehem, she reveals herself – however hiddenly – in her two aspects, taking on the form of Ruth and Orpah.

Our text has explained (p. 34, "The Change in the Feminine") the parting of the sisters according to the dynamics of a new birth of consciousness. To paraphrase succinctly: The motif of the double figure (here the two sisters) in psychology indicates two aspects of a single archetypal content (image/idea) of the unconscious, which content is on the threshold of consciousness. Because coming into consciousness requires an act of differentiation (distinction into discrete parts), it means that the one image/idea becomes two. One capable (timely) of integration into consciousness, the other not. The other therefore lowers itself back to where it came from, the unconscious.

I would specify that in the examples given in our text – of Cain and Abel, Gilgamesh and Enkidu, Jacob and Essau,

<hr>

[65] I am not writing an essay on psychological theory and so do not add in the text what may be the obvious truth, that in "translating" from one medium to another, it could easily be seen that in Jungian terminology Naomi would be a Self figure and Ruth the anima ... as well as the known "mother/maiden" duo.

Castor and Pollux ... and the two sacrificial goats in the Yom
Kippur ceremony of old! – that the less capable of integration
does not necessarily fall totally into the unconscious but
remains relatively conscious. It becomes the shadow side of
that image/idea that has been integrated. In other words, one
becomes the light and accepted side while the other becomes
the dark, unaccepted side. As such it carries the unconscious
projections, usually considered evil – or at least having a
negative connotation inasmuch as such image/idea has
remained undeveloped.[66] In our story it is obviously Ruth
who represents the integrated aspect of the goddess image
while it is Orpah who returns back to where she came from.

Ruth

It is Ruth who has more energy and vitality (i.e., qualities of
consciousness) as seen in her being the one who *voices* her
devotion, and who is *clearly insistent* on being with Naomi. It
is Ruth who is the benevolent aspect of the goddess, which the
story already lets us know through her name. Our text tells us
"Ruth" comes from the Akkadian "Rutum" meaning "friendship." Kabbalah tells us the identity of Ruth is dove, for her
name spelled backwards (and pronounced "tor") means
"dove" in Hebrew. This is referring to the Talmud which says
that "Because of two good doves, [pure and righteous, Ruth
the Moabite and Na'ama the Ammonite] the Holy One,
blessed be He, had mercy on two great nations [Ammon and
Moab] and did not destroy them"[67] ... and in Kabbalah the

---

[66] This is the standard notion, but I should add that sometimes there is a "bright
shadow"; an image that is not integrated, that carries the talents a particular
consciousness has difficulty in accepting ... and which therefore works in
shadowy ways, even though the associations to it are "positive."

[67] *Book of Ruth*, Rabbi Nosson Scherman, compiled by Rabbi Meir Zlotowitz;
Mesorah Publications, Ltd. New York, 1976.

dove refers to the Sh'chinah, seen also as the dove cum Shulamit in the Song of Songs.

Judging from the fact that the Book of Ruth was written long ago and thereafter received widely and lovingly, one could say, "Ruth has been received" – at least historically. "Femininity has been redeemed" – at least within the conscious constructs of the collective, at least as far as virtue and fidelity and appropriate love-making are concerned. But I ask myself, Has the ideal woman become one who is meekly obedient, without a will of her own? Are we seeing Ruth as too sweet? too good?

An image/idea once integrated into consciousness can become, over a period of time, stale and flat. No longer vital, no longer *really* conscious. This is not the fault of the image. The image should not be discarded as so much stale flat beer, but should be revitalized since the mythical meaning in itself did not die – it still is brewing in the cellar of our collective *sub*consciousness. To revitalize the image we have to look at it afresh ... and we have to find as well that part of it which was *not* integrated: the shadow side – in this case Orpah. But first ... but first ... let's not throw away the ideal of Ruth. This is, after all, one complete image – the goddess, dark and light.

Few of us can say we've "arrived" with all of our Ruth virtues in good working order. There is always much waiting to be discovered in that which we thought well known. The devotion to Naomi, which some might call blind, actually sees with the eyes of a visionary, her fateful role – albeit as yet unbeknownst to her, and therefore all the more loving. Ruth knew with an insistent surety – far from meek – to whom she belonged, and thereby what destiny she must follow. This love has remained the epitome of selfless devotion through the ages and is still calling to us, still deeply touching our hearts.

"Do not urge me to leave you, to turn back and not follow you. For wherever you go, I will go; wherever you lodge I will lodge; your people shall be my people, and your God my God. Where you die, I will die, and there I will be buried. Thus and more may the Lord do to me if anything but death parts me from you."[68]

How many of us can follow so "blindly" – without knowing what is in store for us – our true vision, our own calling, our own love? We are called by so many other worldly voices to do this-that-and-the-other. In our quest for consciousness and liberation, we have become victims of the multitudes of pundits declaring The Way – never mind the smaller duties of life shouting for our attention (what a friend of mine recently called "the nuts and bolts of daily living") keeping us from the "small still voice," the "soft murmuring sound."

Ruth and Naomi share in this quality of commitment to their destiny, connected as they are with being the Upper and the Lower Mother, the upper and lower Sh'chinah. This kabbalistic understanding explains the unity which our text refers to as their "mystical identity." My early image of Naomi as "leading lady" plays out very well in this "Upper Mother and Sh'chinah" (Binah) comparison, as do my descriptions of her as the "ground of Being" and the "creative Place" ... the "animating force," as "pivotal point," the "hub of the wheel"[69] at one in itself while radiating out of itself ... initiating the initiative of the characters. It was to my great delight when I later read in the Zohar Ruth that Naomi is identified as Binah.[70]

What does seem a bit strange is that when Naomi eventually receives it is with a passive, almost absent-minded acceptance, Ruth's astounding declarations of love. Perhaps an automatic motherliness. This is not so according to the *Midrash Rabbah*, where Naomi is playing a wisely cautious

---

[68] Ruth 1:16-17, *Tanakh*,

[69] This actually would not be correct in Kabbalah for Binah is always in union with Hochma, the means of her creation. There is an image of the s'firot tree as a wheel, and its center is Tiferet ... as it is in the tree.

[70] As I already mentioned, that book does not follow the meaning of our text – at least not specifically – but is about the soul's [as world soul] process of redemption in the afterlife.

role in testing Ruth's commitment to come into a new religion that would demand far more of her than she was accustomed to in the old. However, reading the story as is, I see more of that Naomi I spoke of (as also in our text) who is as yet unaware of her having received the new feminine, the lost dove. True as it may be that her not seeing clearly was due to her immersion in her bitterness, it may just as well be true that this automatic compassion, a woman's way, is the very virtue that allows for the more individuated commitment which she shortly thereafter displays to Ruth and to her son's memory – which in biblical times would be the same as saying, to the tradition and thereby to her people as a whole.

This is a religious commitment – and therein lies our need to receive Ruth, as well as to be a Ruth and a Naomi, ever and again. "Religious" need not mean to a particular dogma, but is religious in the meaning of lovingly committed to an ideal that transcends – but is intimately connected with – a personal devotion. A religious view sees the larger picture and one's place in it. The Book of Ruth is not a love story based on personal desire alone. The beauty of the story is just in its simplicity of appearing to be a personal story of love and at the same time allowing that to be the carrier of the transcendent meaning.

Best of all, the story does not pontificate. It "only" displays the instinctual womb-wisdom of mother-daughter being – which then allures into being, the masculine initiative. We see this initiation into action so beautifully on the threshing floor, under Naomi's instruction to the beautiful Ruth.

There is even a phrase in Kabbalah, *"mayin de nukba,"* or *mayin nukvin* (Aramaic for "waters of the feminine") which refers to the feminine (Sh'chinah or humanity) sexual allure in order to arouse Tiferet-Yesod into uniting with her, arousing upward to bring downward the flow, not being the receptive only. This is what Kabbalah calls "the drawing down of the King." This is actually a theme throughout the Zohar, 'Through an action below, an action above is aroused,' through an action on the human plane, the divine will be aroused ... in our case Ruth's and Boaz's actions as arousing the divine response, via the cunning of Naomi. In doing this she brings about the flow within God – then flowing into the world below. An act of redemption.

Sadly or fortunately, we know that redemption, as far as we've come in our world and in our beings as mortals, is temporary ... and *tempus fugit* ... and *mutit!* With the mutations in the winds of time our archetypal images may undergo transmutations, with the archetypal core (the archetype as such) retaining its life.[71] Redemption is at hand (or not) ever and again. Though Ruth may be alive and well, we in our cultural mutations and transformations have need now to review the new form of the feminine as including Orpah, that aspect which didn't make it way back then, that which had been cast out, what I referred to in the beginning of this essay as Redeeming Orpah. She has come into our lives already, in various shapes, under various names. We have seen here how Receiving Ruth can be read both ways, she was received and she receives. Now let's see how returning Orpah is read.

Orpah

"Turn back, each of you, to her mother's house. ... See, your sister-in-law has returned to her people, and her gods." (Ruth 1:8 and 1:15)

The daughter who followed Naomi's advice, but did not follow Naomi, eventually came to be considered as evil. The

---

[71] There are differing notions on this: Does the archetype change – or does only the image change? – or do we perceive changes due to *our* mutations? But then do we have an "our" outside of archetypal reality? Perception may be all. That the archetype *moves* is all I can say with a surety. Otherwise I'm in the realm of metaphysics and the New Physics.

Talmud writes of her harlotry and the Zohar Ruth goes so far as to have her committing the ultimate sin, separating the name (the unity) of God.[72] The calendar picture I loved so well in my childhood held no such condemnation. It showed a very sad Orpah ... not bad ... not wanting to leave ... but somehow doing that anyhow. I always felt sorry for her. I always wondered what happened to her.

Before looking for her I want to give some commonplace negative judgments their fair share. There is something about her, after all, that is commonplace. She goes back home.

It is true, simply a fact, that she is that side which just can't come along to the new land. She may personify our doubts, doubts, doubts; holding back out of lack of faith, lack of courage. Certainly lack of adventure (though it is not adventure that Ruth is after). If I were to witness her non-action (rather than her sadness as seen in the painting) I might very well yell at her "C'mon girl, shake it!", impatient with her wishy-washyness. Am I being harsh? Should I consider that she may be that cautious side of us which takes into careful consideration the practicalities of life, leaning on the conservative side? ... and deciding that her future is better looked after in the past. Maybe she has obligations back there. She may be just as dutiful as Ruth. But to what? I cannot escape thinking she's playing it too safe – and since I don't, I find myself condemning her (i.e., my shadow side – but then she *is* the shadow in our text's interpretation). Out of fairness I have to admit that 'safe' is not a bad thing; but bad in this instance for it is just this instance that is begging for new consciousness. A person who slinks back home, to mama's house and mama's gods ... no matter how practical or necessary such a step may

---

[72] In the Zohar Ruth, the family Elimelech are represented b y the letters of the tetragrammaton, the holy name of God, "YHVH" (the letters being yud, heh, vav, heh) There are two letters "heh" and the first refers to Naomi and the second to the daughters, Ruth and Orpah. "Vav" refers to the sons and "yud" to the father. Therefore when Orpah leaves, she is parting, taking out and separating the "heh" from the name.

sound ... is not about to find new consciousness. Orpah is the side of us that cannot live up to challenge, that cannot be put on the spot, that cannot face the unknown, but prefers what is safe and sound in one's own habitat, leading the habitual life.

What is interesting is that her type of women has the sympathy of the collective, is called "realistic," for she is its voice – being a creature of habit she is the voice of the status quo. Therefore again I say, we are not reading a story about the beauty of the stable side of life in the Book of Ruth; we are witnessing the necessity of the integration of the unknown here – the development of consciousness. Very unstabilizing – demanding often that we risk all.

I've just described the Orpah aspect as a fearful person. This however is not what I've had in mind as the Orpah who has been a shadow figure for our culture (although to each his own shadow) and not at all what Orpah has come to represent to us when reading the Talmud and Zohar Ruth. I wrote of her as "stuck" ... whereas they write of her as downright evil. It is this kind of "bad woman" of which they speak that has been the dark side of the goddess for our Western civilization.

What I wrote above are judgments I've made on the level of the "everyday," not the archetypal dark goddess, but more of our personal issues. I was trying to understand the outcome of this process of discrimination of consciousness as shown in our story, this falling back of half of it into the unconscious ... and what it holds for us to learn in our daily modes. In other words, I was moralizing. This has its place. In receiving Ruth we are obliged to know what the leaving of Orpah means. One of those meanings is fear of change, fear of commitment. "Evil" or not, going back to what she had already been speaks for itself.

Looking at the story as story, the only thing we can say for a surety about Orpah is that in the Book of Ruth she is not the developing side of the feminine, she is the retreating side. There is no condemnation (or even negative judgment) here for that is simply how the new content of consciousness manifests itself: pairs of opposites, one in the other out – one new the other old – one in the light the other in the shadow. Just so. All we can really say then is: It was not the time for Orpah to follow Naomi, it *was* the time for Orpah to live in Moab. This attitude allows the story to live its own life and so I prefer it.

The way the story of Orpah lived in the later consciousness of the Talmud and continued by Kabbalah, was the natural way the rejected aspect of the new content of consciousness plays itself out: it became the carrier of the shadow. If Ruth is righteous, Orpah is evil. Not a surprise. Moab is the *sitra achra*, the side of evil ... and ... since Moab is the land of the pagan goddess, and (in accordance with our text) only her redeeming virtues have been brought into Israel, then of course what remains are the dregs. Lively dregs however! Holding within themselves the robust wine of which they were a part.

I want to consider here all of the damnations thrown upon Orpah – true in their purpose and their time – and then see if she isn't just that very scapegoat we spoke of, the goat of atonement, led into the desert, to the place of origins ... so that we may be renewed by her, through her, with her. That, in a sentence, is my 'thesis' on Orpah.

As I did as a child, the talmudists and kabbalists did in their wisdom wonder on whatever became of Orpah. According to the *midrashim* when Orpah returned to Moab she became a harlot.

> "Scarcely had she separated from Naomi when she abandoned herself to an immoral life. (and her comes the interesting part) But with God nothing goes unrewarded. For the four miles which Orpah traveled with Naomi, she was recompensed by bringing forth four giants, Goliath and his three brothers ..."

We see the same in another section,

"Orpah had led a life of unspeakable infamy. Her son Goliath was jeered at as 'the son of a hundred fathers and one mother.' But God lets naught go unrewarded, even in the wicked. In return for the forty steps Orpah had accompanied her mother-in-law Naomi, Goliath the Philistine, her son, was allowed to display his strength and skill for forty days ..."

Here we see that though she is heartily condemned, paths are left open to consider her with respect.

Not only the sons of Orpah waged war against Israel, and were killed by David, but she herself was killed by David. Restitution and settling affairs between the grandsons of Ruth and Orpah ... the answer to the split from Ruth is here seen as *total*: Orpah must be done away with, and is[73]. The results of God's reward was short lived. In psychological terms, the shadow was utterly rejected.

According to that writer, her name Orpah was actually Harapha (in Hebrew lettering the two names are almost identical) which means grits. When she turned her neck (*oreph* – considered as the meaning of her name)...

"... upon her mother-in-law and returned to her place in the land of Moab ... she was unchaste and they did not welcome her, so she went to the land of the Philistines. Everyone pounded her like grits because she gave herself to prostitution. ... Orpah reverted immediately to her sin and perversion."[74]

Also in the Zohar Ruth, her original name was Cherpah, meaning Disgrace.

What appears to be a flat condemnation of Orpah has its nuances. In the *midrashim* there is the "reward" granted by God, however double-edged ... but stronger than that, there is, in the Zohar Ruth, within the person of Orpah herself, that quality which is of Ruth – the same soul stuff. This would be based on the myth of them being sisters, daughters of King

---

[73] Louis Ginzberg, *Legends*, vols. IV and VI.
[74] From three different sections in, *The Mystical Study of Ruth*.

Eglon of Moab ... and in "modern" thinking it is based on the psychological concept of pairs of opposites, *within* the single archetypal image of goddess. The Zohar Ruth understands this even if not in our Jungian terms.

Ruth and Orpah both belong to the s'fira of Malchut. (the Sh'chinah) *Both* of them! In addition, they are both of the same soul quality, belonging to the *nefesh* part of the soul.

Soul in Kabbalah

In Kabbalah the soul is divided into three parts, *nefesh, ruach* and *neshama*. They are in a progressing order, but interdependent inasmuch as the higher rests upon – does not overcome! – the lower. To describe very simply: *Nefesh* is the soul of everyman, it is innate; the source of our animal vitality and governing all the psycho-physical functions. *Ruach* (a word usually translated as spirit) is the acquired soul belonging to those who have developed their intellectual and religious sensibilities, the spiritual side of life. *Neshama*, the most intricate, belongs to that person who has developed through study of Torah and following its commandments. "... it opens his higher powers of apprehension, especially his ability to mystically apprehend the Godhead and the secrets of the universe. Thus, it is the intuitive power that connects mankind with its Creator."[75]

These progressions of soul from the innate, to the acquired, to the truly superior are indeed progressions of value but one does not take the place of the other, they are always interdependent parts of a whole, i.e., our being. The body's good care allows the energy for study, while study invigorates the body. Even in the innate *nefesh*, of "animal vitality" body and mind are not divided, it is our psycho-physical functioning. "It is the source of man's capacity to think, to imagine, to dream, to

---

[75] Gershom Scholem, *Kabbalah*

contemplate,"[76] i.e., psyche. So here, psyche and soma are one.

The Zohar Ruth, taking this system from an earlier kabbalistic work, had its variances. When they, *nefesh* and *ruach,* work properly together *neshama* comes in to unite them, and carry them to the supernal realm. One could say in this system that it is uniting the self with the Self, i.e., with the transcendent. The "downfall" here is that the Zohar Ruth DIVIDED *nefesh* into two: the intellectual and the animal ... the two that had been one in the previous (and later) systems. When the *nefesh* is functioning on the animalistic side, the *ruach* is not sustained, with the result that the *neshama* is thereby forsaken.

According to the Zohar Ruth, Naomi is the *neshama* (being Binah), while Ruth and Orpah are both *nefesh* (being Malchut)... with the difference being that Ruth represents the intellectual side and Orpah the animal side. This is where the dichotomy of Ruth/Orpah fits into the unity of Malchut. Is this not just the same as the Jungian definition of the dynamics of an archetypal content on the threshold of consciousness?! Malchut (the Sh'chinah) is one, divided into two – as she comes into a new consciousness in the Book of Ruth. One is "good" and accepted (intellectual *nefesh,*) the other is "bad" and rejected (animal *nefesh*).

The split between intellectual and animal is made total in the Zohar Ruth, though one cannot say 'absolute' since both are aspects of the Sh'chinah. Nonetheless the unity of God is broken asunder ... by Orpah's animal *nefesh*. The split in the unity must be healed.

*
* *

This outcome was to be expected, wasn't it. Not just the splitting, which is natural, but that the animal side is considered to be the side of evil ... despite the fact of there having

[76] Adin Steinsaltz, *The Thirteen Petalled Rose,* trans. Yehuda haNegbi, Basic Books, Inc., New York, 1980

once been the wisdom that body and soul are one. The animal side is the side that still (or again) had to be overcome. That was "then"... and in some individual cases "now." But I shall be speaking historically. If we were to write the story now we would probably be having the intellectual *nefesh* as the one that is over attenuated and causing the split. This is generally how we proclaim the problem of today.

It is as if we have come full circle back to the original Book of Ruth, beginning as it does with a famine in the land which (in the interpretation of our text) is due to the lack of the earth goddess, the erotic "animal" side of life; sexy, abundant, loving and fructifying. And it was just those qualities which are returned in the person of Ruth! ... likened to "The woman of valor" in proverbs.

The Zohar Ruth was written in the 13th century ... some two thousand years after Ruth. The different *midrashim* I quoted were written earlier, but still of a sufficient period of time to have come around, once again, to having the spirit in the ascendant in such a way as to look down upon the animal side of life. There may be outer historical reasons for this (such as the diaspora, not being allowed to live on one's own land, disconnected from earth, having to combat animalistic behavior in one's enemies, compensating land-loss and loss of the material Temple, with spiritual pursuits) as well as inner psychic dynamics functioning according to psyche's own mode (such as the image of the upward spiraling path of consciousness – seeming to come around to the same point, same issues, but on a higher level). Whether it is outer historical or inner psychological (probably being both and then some) the outcome looks the same: the animal side is denigrated.

Not always, but often in our cultures, the woman has represented the animal and body side of life while man represents spirit. This is one of the many reasons for women carrying the brunt of the prejudice – since "body" does carry it – since "body" is what weighs us down, holds us back, reminds us of our mortality and makes us too, too heavy. Our human nature is always and always flying high, reaching for the stars it would seem – at the cost of the body.

As regards men being equated with spirit and women with body I should add, that here in the Zohar Ruth it is not only the feminine that is representative of the attenuated "animal" side but her husband, Chilion, and he doesn't even rate as much amplification in the legends as does Orpah, thereby showing either a greater valuation of the feminine ... or ... showing that the feminine is more problematic, that issue with which we must deal. This is why "she" captured the imagination.[77]

On page 114 I asked why I had allowed my gleeful imagination to turn Naomi into a wild nature woman and then asked rhetorically what this said about our culture, have we all become so overburdened with civilization. Now, in the name of redeeming Orpah, I can look at that.

What is Orpah not? If she is the dark side of Ruth then she is neither obedient nor selfless ... nor sexually virtuous. Yes, I believe I've seen her around quite a bit. If the animal is held down too long it becomes restive or rambunctious, or sick. Also, when the animal is not truly integrated into our human consciousness we continue the imprisonment either by repression or by identification ... acting out in the animal ways ... which poor animal is neurotic in itself, having for so long been chained. These are extremes, but not so rare. Also not so rare is the woman who is not split between the Ruth and Orpah poles, who is at one with her spirit and her animal animating instincts, but this type does not pose itself as the "problem of our times."

I remember a case of a woman whose animal was not sick, but was frantic. She was one of those who kept the animal

---

[77] There are other men, in the Midrash as well, representing animal base instinctuality, such as Essau – who in Kabbalah is also considered as coming from the left side, the side of evil – another of the pairs of opposites.

imprisoned despite the fact that she never would have dreamed (except that she did) she would be guilty of such. She "knew" better. She considered herself to be her own woman, very liberated and up to date on body care and holistic healing. She looked strong and healthy. She was a successful business woman, an entrepreneur of trade shows in which she participated, on stage, presenting.

What she presented in our first session was a very intelligent and likable person, albeit somewhat driven. During the session I felt an increasing pressure in my chest and in the entire room, building up until it seemed I could almost physically hear poundings and sense an explosion. I didn't put this into words for myself I simply noted it. I was carefully listening to her words which held no such atmosphere. She was poised and articulate. At the end of the session I knew, simply for my own sake, that I could not be within the confines of four walls with all of that pounding energy building up. I suggested to her that we have our next session at the beach. I lived and worked in Santa Monica at that time, by the ocean, so it seemed a likely place to go. She happily agreed for she felt at home by the sea. I confess that these years later I do not remember what I made of the reaction I had when I considered it during the interim of our first and second sessions. Whatever it was, it did not hit the mark (perhaps blessedly so) as one can see from the next session.

We sat on the sand in a deserted beach, close to the water. As she spoke and I listened I absent-mindedly let my hand play in the sand. What it did was to produce a magnificent low relief of a horse's head and neck. I was not noticing but she did – suddenly and with a jolt of horrified recognition. "Why did you that?" she asked, almost accusingly. "I don't know," I honestly answered. The sculpture led to her remembering a dream of only the night before, which she then told me.

"I am on stage presenting a show. There is a large and attentive audience and I know I am doing very well, the show is going very well. This is all much as things are in my waking life. But then I know – I don't know how – that while I'm up here being wonderful, there is something terrible, something too awful, happening down below. It is in the basement of the theatre, in my dressing room. A fire has broken out inside my dressing room … and the room is made of iron, thick iron walls and no one can get in. There are horses inside, locked inside! They are beautiful horses, trapped in a raging fire. They are neighing loudly, wildly, reared on their hind legs, their front hoofs pounding frantically at the walls, pounding and pounding to get out."

This was so accurate a picture of her inner reality, that the problem physically manifested itself in my consulting room, though not to her. "Blessedly" I said in referring to my lack of consciousness, for had I been more verbally conscious I might have somehow "explained" it to her. The problem "used" me as a medium of expression (rather than being a wise guide) and this spontaneous way of showing had far more of an impact, causing her to remember her dream and recognizing in it her state of being.

The woman was lucky inasmuch as her horses were healthy. Unlucky in that the split was so severe, so iron clad. The problem had heated up to the point of being on fire, causing her to finally notice the hell her animals were in. Her fiery spirit was turned against her nature.

More often I've seen dreams of sick animals or abandoned animals that come in from the cold wanting, needing, attention. Sometimes it's a wonderful creature presenting itself as a wake-up call. In fact, I cannot think of anyone, including me, who hasn't had such a dream. It is a personal problem and the cultural problem of our day … trailing a long history behind it. The split between outer "successful" adaptation and inner instinctuality became so extreme in our recent history that a whole new science was born to understand and heal it: psychology. It is not always the split between outer adaptation and instinct, rather it is the split between ego and instinct. If we see it as the former than we will always be at odds with one or the other. If it is the latter, then we can have them serve one another for the good of our being, arising as they do from our being, and thereby redounding to the benefit of society.

Our society today is probably the most chaotic, the most plentiful, as ever has appeared in history. Full of possibilities. Full of seeds. Full of shit for that matter. Waste and fertilizer too. Orpah seen as Harapha has come into play here. If she is grits then she is made of seeds … composed of future possibilities. A multitude.

We live at the end of an era, the ruling principle of which has fulfilled its meaning, at least as far as we can now take it, yet which continues running on inertia, spiraling away from the center, into entropy and into a famine in the land … even as we gobble everything in sight. Living in a muddle of outmoded cultures we claim multi-mode as the way, taking comfort in chaos theory and cursing the patriarchy for its linear determinism and monism. At this point we find an easy prey in a patriarchy molded in our image of rationalism and rule. We look back in anger to our origins as we currently wish to see them in the Bible, calling those by the odd name of "Judaeo-Christian" and blaming them for male supremacy and thereby all our ills. We do this damning while painting Woman gold – even while painting her black – coming as she does form a Golden Age.

There! I've let my virulence out. I become frustrated at the proclamations, which confessedly I myself have been proclaiming, when done in a one-sided way. Orpah was damned as base instinctuality, so now as a cure she's adored. Neither damnations nor adorations are the answer, but oh so easy to come by since our culture as a whole has yet to find 'the answer' – the redeeming, individuated, way.

Society discovered (to some degree) that by damning the whore it might succeed in cleaning the streets but it would not be in touch with its own lust. It did touch society however by working in the dark, in obsessive fantasies or compulsive acting itself out. Looking at yesterday's Victorian era we see this clearly, but it still lives ... and in varying degrees this acting out is what we have witnessed, in one way or another, as the hallmark of our times. With all good will many are now trying to redeem the lusty black goddess only to be caught in her swamp. Hard to touch that life-infested mud without being sullied. Impossible in fact, and no doubt a necessary step in the process of becoming conscious of it. Which is to say, sorting out the life therein, not piggy wallowing in it.

We all will be, and are, learning how to play in the mud again. This I see as the return of Orpah, for I cannot make a specific picture of this woman of pounded seeds. She must remain for us all that which we have not yet known in our pagan natures ... coming as she does from Moab. Playing in moist earth's mud seems a very good place to start.

CHAPTER 8

Sifting and Sorting the Shadows
The Likeness of Lilit and the Sh'chinah

In an effort to know and picture this goddess blackness one of her many icons has been Lilit. I remember being quite surprised, some 22 years ago or so, when I saw a new publication, a feminist magazine called "Lilith." The popularity of the name has grown since then. In the name of my continuing surprise I would like to draw some distinctions between Lilit and the Sh'chinah – to whom belongs Orpah – for I believe a grave mistake is being made here which could backfire if we don't treat Lilit with caution, and grant Lilit her immutable evil.

The following are the reasons I've come across for the lauding of Lilit. First off, she is lumped with all the other goddesses who represent earth, sexuality and fertility, the main feature being that she, as they, has been rejected by society ... which rejection is taken to be the reason she is considered evil. The other feature is her self assertion and her independence. This is taken from the now popular story that she refused to have sex with Adam if she could not be on top, which he claimed as his priority, which she disputed on the grounds that he had no priority over her since they were both made of dust and on the same day. She left him through her magic. She pronounced the ineffable name of God, flew into the air, landed at the Red Sea where she dallied with her demon friends. Adam pleaded with God to bring her back and when she refused, she was threatened that if she did not return, hundreds of her demon children (which she birthed daily) would be killed. Her response was to declare that she preferred this punishment to life with Adam.

One can readily see how feminism gets a kick out this story. There is something black-humorously gratifying in Lilit's staunch stance against "the men."

Here is what Lilit looks like: She has a beautiful woman's face and body but large bird claws for feet. She has wings. It is said, "She is a beautiful woman above but sheer fire below" Here are some of the facts about Lilit's "personality." She is a demon. She does not live in relation to any human being, rather she lives off of human beings; she is a succubus. Her sexuality is for her own power, not for love. It is true she gives birth to hundreds of children per day, and could be seen therefore as a symbol of fertility, were it not for the fact that she cannot give birth without stealing human semen. Furthermore, she has no milk in her breasts to nurse her hundreds of demon children. She is a seductress who lures men away from their wives ... she kills women in childbirth. She strangles babies. Maybe she eats them. She sucks blood, she sucks semen – she sucks the life forces. A very fine demon.

In a previous chapter I called her the "heroine of self-authority." She answers to no one ... at least not that I've heard of. Another way she's viewed is through the pity she supposedly has earned by the patriarchy's refusal to allow her top position. Pity?! I'd guess she'd throw it back in our face ... and maybe has ... or she's eaten it. In our climb to emancipation we may have stumbled, falling backwards to the Victorian refrain of "She's more to be pitied than censured." "She must be integrated into consciousness – valued as feminine power and sexuality – rescued from the chains that bound her to the *sitra achra* – reverse the appellation of 'evil' – for how mistaken those name-callers are!" Thus goes the refrain of those who want to rescue Lilit. I am all for the song, I would just rather sing it to Orpah (and other deserving figures), to whom it would be more fitting.

I'll point up again that we are taking the characters in myth and religion as images of an archetype. As such these images form the basis of our psyche, structuring our perceptions, forming our being as human. Jung's terse explanation was 'the archetype is the way the instinct pictures itself.' In other words, archetypal images are *a priori* structures of apperception and not of our making. Even if the image itself is shaped from experience its existence is founded upon a basic, *a priori,* force of life. We therefore should approach these images with respect. They have a life. And we don't even know the whole of it.

It is true that, true to the times, Lilit is making an appearance all by herself – but if we go along and conjure up Lilit we must remember that she brings a real history with her which is not subject to our conscious constructs. In her stories, we see that Lilit lives, and *rules* (with her male counterpart, Sama'el) in the *sitra achra,* on the other side of our created world – *and* is sustained by the Creator, i.e., there is a divine purpose in this realm of evil. This does not diminish, but enhances the fact that she is really and truly Evil … her job is to do evil.

In speaking of differences between Orpah, Sh'chinah, and Lilit, – and their roles in redeeming what has been split asunder – I would like to differentiate between relative and absolute evil, even while knowing my attempts will be sloppy, at best. For one thing, Kabbalah itself has contradictory notions of whether or not the *sitra achra* is relative or absolute. For another, it is extremely difficult to draw clear demarcations in the discrimination of what is, after all, working in the shadows. Folklore on the other hand has no qualms about considering Lilit absolutely evil. A plethora of amulets to protect babies and women in childbirth attests to that.

One very clear demarcation however is that Lilit is a demon and Orpah is a human being. This difference is not to be underrated.

The Zohar has evil in a realm totally its own, that has its own hierarchy, a counterworld to the s'firot world of divine emanations – imitating it. The *sitra achra*, is this totally other side. It is made up of shells, or husks, *klippot*, the dregs of creation, the dross of what had been the "sacred gold" ... "in which the holy is either nonexistent, or present only as a spark, concealed and glowing within the dross."[78] Even these aspects of evil contain the "divine sparks" by which contact can be made for the purpose of redemption. However, this is more true of the Hassidim's interpretations than it is of the Zohar. It is all very fluid. Absolute evil mingles and changes shape with relative and redeeming evil. But in itself "it" never becomes "good."

To give Orpah her body – and to show an identity with Lilit – I shall have to speak again of the Sh'chinah and her dark aspect. (I am speaking here of Orpah as the human manifestation of the Sh'chinah, as discussed in the previous section; Ruth being the light side, Orpah the dark. The Sh'chinah's dark side is not Orpah the human woman, but Orpah is the dark side of the Sh'chinah, as she was manifested in this particular story.) In the section on the Sh'chinah I spoke of a destructive side coming out when she is filled with too much Din ... and further than this, her combining aspects of the dark goddess of death when she falls into the *sitra achra*, the realm of Lilit, becoming very much like her. This more extreme stage is caused by human erring and sin, which causes her separation from Tiferet. She leaves the realm of holiness and resides in the realm of Satan and evil, becoming a shell, a *klipah*. Here are some quotes from the Zohar that describe the Sh'chinah in such changes:

"When the righteous multiply in the world, *Knesseth Yisra'el* [the *Shekhinah*] emits sweet fragrances [like a rose], and is blessed by the holy king, and her face is radiant. But when the wicked

---

[78] Gershom Scholem, "Sitra Ahra: Good and Evil In The Kabbalah," *Mystical Shape*

people increase in the world, *Kenesseth Yisra'el*, as it were, does not emit sweet fragrances, but tastes of the Other, bitter Side. Of this state it is written, 'He has cast down from heaven the earth' [Lam. 2:1], and her face is darkened."

One passage describes her in images that had been used to describe Lilit:

> "A thousand mountains loom before her, and all are like a puff of wind to her. A thousand mighty streams rush past her, and she swallows them in one swallow. Her nails reach out to a thousand and seventy sides; her hands grasp on to twenty-five thousand sides; nothing eludes her rule on this side or the other [*Sitra Achra*]. How many thousands of potencies of judgement are grasped in her hair …" (Zohar, I, 223b)

It is said of her that "her feet go down to death," a phrase used for Lilit – and – 'she becomes fire and consumes all that is below her,' also reminiscent of Lilit.

Another passage goes so far as to call her the mother of Lilit and Na'amah! (Na'amah being the other main female demon.)

I quote all of this for three reasons. One is to show the ambivalence and vascillations of the Sh'chinah and the second is to show how this female image has the qualities of power and darkness that "we" are wanting to claim in the name of our wholeness, seeing them in the form of Lilit – and not surprisingly since they do belong to her. But she is not whole. She is only evil. The Sh'chinah is Good and Evil. If we are hell bent on gaining our own darkness we must be careful as to where we seek it … unless of course we want to become utterly dark (which is not whole). If we want to "redeem" Lilit from the dark then we are contradicting ourselves. The Sh'chinah on the other hand moves between the realms. This is the third reason: to point out motility and change. Can transformation even be attempted without those?

The Gateway to Redemption, the Creator and Sovereign of the world, the Beneficent mother, the Lover of God and mankind, the Radiance of God ... all of these attributes of the Sh'chinah can turn into their opposite when she becomes *Ilana de Mota*, the Tree of Death, in her separation from Tiferet. She can live in both realms – at home in one, in exile in the other – but partaking wholly of each when in them! No such change, no such vacillation – no such *flexibility* – is to be seen in the character of Lilit. In considering this my question was: is it Lilit who is being described as the cast out feminine, here called Orpah, or is it the dark side of the Sh'chinah? I've answered my question, haven't I.

No doubt there is an outcast side of womanhood calling for recognition and redemption. The image of the three mothers, Naomi, Ruth and Orpah, the three wandering widows, the three barren women, is so poignant to me as an image of woman in her totality being totally bereft. One midrash says they are barefoot and in rags! They have returned to us, in our day, back in their former unredeemed state. We all have sympathy for we all are part of this poverty; lack and bereavement. But how is the best way to help?

I am still functioning under our assumption that to redeem means to make whole again that which has become split off. I do not see that Lilit has been split off from anything, she is totally what she is. Not the dark side of a good being. She is not in exile, as the Sh'chinah can be. She lives in her own realm of the *sitra achra*, never captured. The only casting out has been done by herself, according to her own "good," i.e., complete, unity – her own determination to be as she is. Humanity's actions and opinions do not make Lilit bad, do not split Lilit from herself or her realm ... as it does the Sh'chinah.

I am still following the principle of pairs of opposites being part of a whole. Not only has Lilit not been split off (or cast out) of what was once a totality, she is that very *principle of separation* that redemption wants to heal. She separates loving unions and she separates from life and she separates herself from relationship. As shown earlier, loving unions on earth cause the union between God and His Sh'chinah, which brings benefit to the world below. Lilit's being a seductress does far more than harm the marriage of the human couple.

I realize that it is just this side of her that makes her an icon for independence for those who want to say, "I don't have to be 'good,' you can't make me, I'm my own boss, I don't have to be a mother, I don't have to be a wife, I can be whatever kind of sexiness and sexuality I so desire," etc. etc. But this is just where I see Lilit as gaining the upper hand, and just where I see our failure as not integrating those qualities we so desire. We're being duped by Lilit, not rescued. Women have become assertive, but often at the cost of their love-life. That needn't be the case, but we won't know how to do it if we are using Lilit as a model. Also, women have claimed their sexuality, but again often at the cost of their love life if sex is pursued indiscriminately … as Lilit does. This is not our animal nature. Animals don't do that.

The sacred prostitute is another image that has become very popular in the name of reclaiming our sexuality.[79] It should be remembered however that she was performing a sacred act, in service to the love goddess, and not being the profane prostitute, also in existence in those days. When we make that discrimination in our love-making then all is in its place. But when reveling in sexuality is lauded as reclaiming our animal natures, let's remember the mating rituals of animals. Most animals have a ritual of seeking out, and sorting out, the chosen mate and then making love in a behavior which takes its time before the actual penetration. (This is not always the case with our domesticated dogs, ruined no doubt by millennia of human contact.) I am reminded of a camping trip in the Sinai where friends and I stopped to watch the mating of two camels. They were oblivious to us, being wrapped up in each other … almost literally. They were necking. Two long necks,

---

[79] R. Schärf Kluger is largely responsible for this from the seminars she gave on Gilgamesh in Zürich beginning in the 40's.

arched and intertwining, this way and that, in and out, so slowly, such grace. This went on and on and on – a ballet of graceful undulating intertwinings, apparently enjoyed for their own beauty. Not being as sophisticated as they in love making, we got bored and left.

Too often, when claimed in the name of Lilit, our stance for self expression and independence is being accomplished under the aegis of Lilit's *coldness*. At best it is petulant and self indulgent, at worst it is truly destructive … to one's integrity and one's relations. It uses people. It sucks out the life forces. Lilit does not represent that animal spirit, the warmth that is wanting to enter our consciousness.

The picture of Orpah is that she is split apart from Ruth. Both are the Sh'chinah … and the Sh'chinah as we've seen can be light and dark. Orpah is the shadow side that carried the quality of the dark goddess, the quality of sexiness and pagan instinctuality. She is that side we are wanting to claim as our own. She may come under the grip of Lilit … just as the Sh'chinah can … but she is not a Lilit herself. As for self-authority, Orpah made her decision to be on her own, not to follow, but to be a "harlot" … and this did not come from coldness or from lack of humanity; just witness her tears. She was sad to leave. Somehow she had to. She is the woman in the shadows who needs to be embraced again. She is the side of the Sh'chinah who once again, who ever and again, needs our attention so that we may be reunited with our personal totality and the transcendent totality of life. That is the Sh'chinah's function, to mediate between holy and divine. Lilit's function is to break mediation … to split asunder union.

One of the theses of our text, and of Kabbalah, and of Jung, is that the Other Side of evil is necessary in the process of consciousness and individuation (redemption). By having the faith or courage to face the other side we can bring back, or find for the first time, parts of ourselves to make up the whole. Ourselves coming into our Self. If so what's the difference between bringing in Lilit from the Other Side and bringing in Orpah from Moab, which represents the Other Side? I've already suggested that it is Orpah's humanity. Humanity relating to our humanity. The other reason is that the Sh'chinah (of which Orpah is the human reflection) is the function of mediation – whereas Lilit is the function of separation. Lilit *belongs* in the *sitra achra*. It is her home, her palace, her realm; she is meant to be there. It's where she works best. How arrogant to think we can "save" her from it, or that she can be "used" to save ourselves. That makes her smaller than she is. The archetypal image is autonomous, not a tool. How dangerous to think we can dwell there. Only our split off consciousness could make such arrogant assumptions. The rejected feminine needs redemption *from* the darkness of the unconscious, but the darkness of the unconscious (of which Lilit is the personified feminine image) does not need rescuing! Where would we be without it?

Looked at from the perspective of the *sitra achra* we could see that any attempt to bring Lilit into consciousness would be anathema to the proud Lilit!

Anathema to the function of that archetypal image of total Otherness. And most certainly absurd, inasmuch as archetypes in themselves don't need redemption! It is altogether different if we ask, Is the archetype calling to be made manifest? If we are at all aware of it then it already is on the threshold, meaning it "wants" to be brought into consciousness. But to what end? All archetypal functions are not the same. If they present themselves and we must accept willynilly (which is sometimes the case, the new consciousness being beyond us) than we must keep our eyes open and not do the dictating … making an archetypal image into the poster child of our desires. Lilit is not a model to be followed – unless of course one adheres to a satanic cult and then truly discovers in horror the autonomy of the archetype. That *we* need redemption doesn't mean that Lilit does. We, in *our* lack of consciousness, have confused images, mistaking one for the other.

Archetypes are not models they are psychic functions. What is the function of Lilit? I've already described her as the principle of separation, as I've already described the function of the Sh'chinah to be the principle of mediation. Our religions and our psychologies tell us that the first is evil, the second is good. But – if evil is necessary in the scheme of things, what purpose does Lilit serve? If she is the principle of separation she is also the principle of consciousness! Just like her consort Satan. Consciousness divides and makes distinctions between this and that. As we have seen in the "this and that" of Ruth and Orpah. The consequence is that one side returns to the unconscious where it falls into the shadows. *That's* the part that needs redemption … not the function of which it is an outcome! And what better function to serve this process than the principle of mediation, the Sh'chinah. In this way Lilit has her hand as the instigator of consciousness. Even of the Sh'chinah – who can fall under her sway. This is just the way Jung in *Answer to Job*, and Rivkah Schärf Kluger in *The Development of Satan in the Old Testament* spoke of the function of Satan in the development of humanity and God Himself (as the Sh'chinah is God). Nowhere was it suggested that Satan should be a role model! The Sh'chinah and Lilit are the means – Orpah is the subject of our redeeming and redemption. The way is ours.

I believe that Lilit represents an *a priori* evil, total in itself, that truly exists and *must* exist in order for us to know the place of evil – not in order for us to rescue Lilit. One cannot, should not, rescue evil out of evil. Where would we be without Lilit as evil? We would be robbed! There would be no Other Side. If Lilit is coming into consciousness these days, to what end? Perhaps to make us stand in awe. Fear is the beginning of wisdom, as the Hebrew expression goes and the Hebrew word for 'fear' is also 'awe,' sometimes used as 'respect' for the divine. Fear and trembling before God. If viewed properly she reminds us, or teaches us, what is awful. To make us aware, conscious, to make us remember that there is the Other Side, not to be toyed with, though we may have to be touched by it. To remember our humility, our humanity, that we after all are the ones made of humus. In this way one may say she leads to redemption, for she is the dark side of the Sh'chinah and she does carry the magic touch.

In Kabbalah there are numerous and beautiful passages describing the Sh'chinah as the Torah. In Gematria (numerology), the numerical equivalence of different words indicates an inner identity. "Lilit" is the numerical equivalent of "Torah"!

CHAPTER 9

Completing the Circle

Have we left poor Orpah in the cold, still waiting to be brought back into the fold? There is no one way to say how she is to be brought in ... except to value once again what had been denigrated, what often still is denigrated. To look with open eyes at all we consider "primitive" in a woman. Not just that nature woman who runs with the wind, that I identified with in an earlier chapter, but her opposite: the slow moving and gestating woman who carefully chews her cud – knowing how to digest the outer world. Both the horse and the cow are necessary components of our animal womanhood ... to say nothing of lions and tigers – our feline, night wise, prowling selves.

It is apparently easier to accept the lusty woman (at least in our stated valuations) than it is the slow cud chewing cow. To call someone a cow is an insult – but it certainly wouldn't be in India. There the cow is the sacred image of Kali, the Great and Awesome Mother prevailing over life and death. This energy is not however the image I've had in mind when suggesting to some women to be cows. What I have in mind is a slow, ruminating and graceful creature, moving in a swaying gait, in a quiet pasture of alfalfa and daisies; as antidote to the frenetic pace so many women follow. It appears that the oughts of the patriarchy are at least equaled by the oughts of matriarchy if I'm to judge by the pushing mother within and behind women I've seen. How insulted they are when I ask them, "Why don't you try being a cow?"

In my work in Judea and Samaria, that portion of Israel known in Jordan as the West Bank and to its Arab inhabitants as Palestine, I have met beautiful cows ... and I have been nurtured by them. The Arab women, both the simple and the sophisticated ones I've known, still have that quality called 'primitive.' What a great shame that word has come to carry such a derogatory meaning. It points up the very problem we speak of here. Overreaching one's capacity, doing damage to our animal nature which sustains us. Calling someone primitive sounds like a prejudiced put-down, just as calling a woman a cow does. But I say it with all respect. Even with longing. I was once that cow, but I lost it early on in my adaptation to the Western world. I am afraid I might be sounding like the Colonialist in Kipling when he said, "You're a better man than I, Gunga Din"; a poem I always found highly offensive. However I don't know how else to say it. The quality I see is primitive, is primal, and most of us need that woman to live well again in our being. She is after all what we are trying to reclaim. This primitive woman quality is also true of the Jewish women coming from Arab countries. I am not saying that nervousness doesn't exist in these women. And I am sad to say that the frenetic Western world is all too much taking its hold – nevertheless as a woman too long removed from the grace of the primitive and the cow, I would say there is much there that I gladly remember and much that I need to be reminded of. A wisdom of time and place and grace.

In Israel the *sitra achra* is not only to be found in psychological reality but is clearly manifest in the political and geographical setting as well. The two, psychological and political, are not separated. This has been a great gift and a great difficulty. In my talking about the Arab as Other, I am not talking about projections arising from the personal shadow. I am talking about the physical reality of "the enemy," openly declared as such ... by both sides. And the friendships between the enemy sides. Though not in the majority such friendships between the enemies are more frequent than is thought. They are loving friendships, and difficult, demanding and causing a breadth of consciousness.

I know a woman who lives in the direction toward Moab, in the town named Anata. She and I are friends, each of us from the Other Side of one another. Because of my name, because of the proximity of what was Moab, because of the name of the town, because of her strict Islamic culture being so different than mine ... I am reminded of the Book of Ruth. She and I don't follow one another into conversion but we do promise protection and devotion in friendship. We have sworn and lived, "Whenever there is a war whichever of us finds herself in enemy territory she will be protected by the other." And yet we do not convert to the other's religious or political views. In true friendship we openly declare our disagreements, together trying hard to find the way of recon-ciliation ... without submission on either side. In a way we do "follow" one another, at least in terms of each being a willing student of the other's culture. When I stay in her home or visit her friends and relatives, just as when she is with me and mine, we are very consciously participating as novices, being "inno-cent" in the home of the hostess. Sometimes she's Naomi and I'm Ruth, sometimes it's the other way around. We take turns in being the 'older and wiser' to the 'younger and following.'

As gathered from the section on Lilit, I do not care for the idea of a biblical character, or any archetypal image, being used as a role model. I find that far too heavy-handed and contrived for images that contain such nuance and living subtlety of expression (theirs and ours). Nonetheless, what often happens – and particularly in a land where one is so aware of their personal ancient history – is that these charac-ters make themselves very much present in daily happenings as ancient reminiscences, as a pattern one suddenly and surprisingly finds oneself contained within, no matter how generally configured. The archetype stands behind our daily happenings. (Which is vastly different than trying to make a fit.) My friend is, in our political actuality, the dark and dangerous side for me, as I am for her. The meaning, if not the events, of the characters in the Book of Ruth, help me very much in this play of opposites, belonging (as we say we do) to the same family.

*
* *

For all that I've spoken about the feminine animal soul and its redeeming quality I have not given the masculine its due as containing that same animal intuitive instinctuality. The masculine principle can also be of a type that bridges instinct and spirit, redeeming through his own connection to the unconscious that which has been cast out. "He" appears in dreams and is always such a positive animus ... to men and to women. Very often he's connected to music. I am remembering his appearance in the dream of a woman who worked with me. She was raised a Catholic and had left the church. Not so much from hostility as disappointment. She found her church in the university and in teaching, but she was too intelligent to be fooled into believing academia would continue to carry her spirit. She knew she could never return to the strict and outmoded confines of the church, but being a person with basically a religious nature she was left at loose ends. How to live in the spirit? – and due to some other issues – How to be in the body? What's more, how to reconnect to her family from whom she'd psychologically estranged herself ... not only personal family but her background and underpinnings. She had the following dream which I'll tell as I'll have to paraphrase. Realize that this dream took place 21 years ago, before many of the recent changes in the church.

"I am walking in the countryside and I hear lively jazz played on a horn. It is very good and I follow the sound. From a hill I see a church below and the sound is coming from there. I go to the church and outside there is a great crowd of people. A priest is administering the sacrament, giving Holy Communion to the congregants. I don't want to do that. I do want to hear the music which is coming from very close by. I notice that the main crowd of people are not in front of this priest but to the side of him. I go to see what is there. The music is there. I discover that this is another line for Holy Communion, and everyone has congregated here. Up at the front of the line is a young priest playing wonderful jazz on a trumpet. He is wearing jeans and a torn T-shirt!"

She laughed with joy in telling the dream. She had found her guide, her communion.

Our story of Ruth promises a redeemer coming from such a spirit. David, the descendent of Obed and the progenitor of the Messiah is just such a character, a mixture – often but not always wise and "good" – of animal and spirit. David the sweet singer of songs. The great King David brought back the tabernacle, the Ark of the Covenant – the dwelling place of the Sh'chinah and all the wisdom of the Torah – back to the people of Israel after its exile, held in captivity by the Philistines. He brought it in a procession up to Jerusalem, up to the holy mountain on which the Temple would be built by his son, Solomon. What a glory and majesty that was. And what did he do, this powerful King? He was so filled with joy and triumph that he took off his clothes and danced before the Torah, leading the procession up to Jerusalem. "David whirled with all his might before the Lord; David was girt with a linen ephod. ... thus David and all the House of Israel brought up the Ark of the Lord with shouts and with blasts of the horn ... King David, leaping and whirling before the Lord ..." (II Samuel 6:14-16) What an image. Red-headed David, almost naked and dancing, protector and redeemer of the home of the spirit of the Lord!

Redeeming that which has been cast out is not only bringing back that other half of the single image; it is in itself an act accomplished by a pair of opposites, i.e., masculine and feminine. I do not retreat from my original notion that this is a book guided by the spirit of Woman, of Naomi and Ruth, representing that mothering, nurturing, creating, feminine side of God. But I do remember that without Boaz there would be no redemption! Without the masculine there would have been neither the casting out nor the bringing back ... into the Great Return.

Binah is called T'shuva, meaning both Return and Repentence. She is the Great the Jubilee. As the mother of all the emanations, each one representing an eon, they all at the end will return to her, into her, and from her Creation begins anew. Fifty is the number of Jubilee for it is in the fifty thousandth year that the seven emanations from her, each being six thousand years (culminating in the seventh), will have fulfilled all their cycles. The great Shabbat (7 x 7 = 49) and the time of completion. It will be remembered that Shavu'ot is also a period of completion in 50 weeks ... and it is Shavu'ot that celebrates receiving the Torah, entering into a sacred covenant with God, and in our story Ruth, Naomi and Boaz bringing this about again by receiving what comes from the Other Side – in order to bring all into Redemption.

I am left with a picture different than the one with which I started. It still has Naomi in the center, tall and strong, but this time on either side of her are Ruth and Orpah, Naomi's arms around each woman's shoulders. In the distant background, looming like a protective mountain in soft shades, is Boaz, as if embracing them all.

Bibliography

The Bible text used here is from *Tanakh, the Holy Scriptures*, a new translation by a committee of scholars, from the traditional Hebrew text into idiomatic modern English, published by the Jewish Publication Society, Philadelphia, 1988. In a few instances the translation from the earlier J. P. S. version or the Revised Standard Version has been used where deemed necessary for the sake of clearer understanding of the literal Hebrew rather than its idiomatic rendition.

Albright, W. F. *Archeology and the Religion of Israel,* 1946.
Apuleius, Lucius, *The Golden Ass,* Penguin Books, Harmondsworth, 1950.
Baudissin, W. W., *Adonis und Esmun,* 1911.
Bal, Mieke, *Lethal Love: Feminist Literary Readings of Biblical Love Stories.* 1987.
Bernstein, Moshe J., "Two Multivalent Readings in the Ruth Narrative," Journal for the Study of the O. T. 50, 1991.
Bin Gorion, M. J., *Die Sagen der Juden,* Schocken Verlag, Berlin, 1935.
Brenner, Athalya, *Ruth and Naomi,* A. Oren, Publishers, Ltd., Tel-Aviv, 1988. (Hebrew)
Burnstein, D. J., articles "Incest" in *Encyclopaedia Judaica.,* Berlin, 1934, vol. viii. and vol. x.
Book of Ruth, Rabbi Nosson Scherman, compiled by Rabbi Meir Zlotowitz; Mesorah Publications, Ltd. New York, 1976.
(A) Dictionary of the Bible, ed. J. Hastings, 11th ed., Edinburgh, 1942.
S. R. Driver, "Deuteronomy," *The International Critical Commentary,* Edinburgh, 1902.
Dubin, Lois C., article in the collection *Reading Ruth,* ed. Kates and Reimer, New York, 1994.
Eliade M., *The Myth of the Eternal Return,* Bollingen Series XLVI, Pantheon Books, New York, 1954.

Encyclopaedia Judaica, ed., J. Klatzkin, 10 vols. (through L), Berlin, 1928-1934.

Encyclopaedia Judaica, eds., Cecil Roth, G. Wigoder, Keter, Jerusalem, 1972.

Encyclopaedia of Religion and Ethics, ed. James Hastings, T & T Clark, Edinburgh, 1913.

Epstein, I., Foreword to Midrash Rabbah, vol. 1.

von Franz, Marie-Louise, *On Divination and Synchronicity: The Psychology of Meaningful Chance,* (Original seminar transcribed by Una Thomas), Toronto, Inner City Books, 1980.

Frazer, Sir James George, *The Golden Bough,* 1 volume abridged edition, The Macmillan Company, New York, 1955.

— *The New Golden Bough,* abridged, ed. T. H. Gaster, Criterion Books, New York, 1959.

Freedman H., "Genesis" in *The Soncino Chumash,* ed., A. Cohen, The Soncino Press, Hindhead, Surrey, 1947.

Gaster, Theodor Herzl, *Thespis; Ritual, Myth and Drama in the Ancient Near East,* Doubleday and Company, New York, 1950.

Gesenius, D. Wilhelm, *Handwörterbuch über die Schriften des Alten Testaments,* first ed., F. C. W. Vogel, Leipzig, 1810.

— ed. F. Buhl, ed. 16, Leipzig, 1915.

Ginzberg, Louis, *Legends of the Jews,* 6 vols., 5th ed., Jewish Publication Society, Philadelphia, 1968.

Globe, Alexander, "Folktale Form and National Theme, with Particular Reference to Ruth," in Olshen and Feldman, eds., *Approaches to Teaching the Hebrew Bible as Literature in Translation,* 1989.

Goff, Beatrice, "Syncretism in the Religion of Israel," in *Journal of Biblical Literature,* 58, 1939.

Green, Barbara, *A Study of Field and Seed Symbolism in the Biblical Story of Ruth* (Ph. D, thesis) 1980.

Greenstein, E. L., "On Feeley-Harnik's Reading of Ruth" in S. Niditch, ed., Text and Tradition: *The Hebrew Bible and Folklore,* Semeia Studies, 1990.

Gressman, H., "Dolmen, Masseben und Napflöcher" in ZAW 29, 1909.

Gunkel, H., 1917, "Genesis," in W. Nowack, ed., *Göttinger Handkommentar zum Alten Testament,* Göttingen, 1917.

— 1925, "Ruth," in *Deutsche Rundschau,* 10/105, 1925.

Haller, M., "Die Fünf Megilloth," in O. Eissfeldt, ed., *Handbuch zum Alten Testament,* Tübingen, 1940.

Harel Fish, A., "Gishah Structuralistith l'sipurre Ruth v'Boaz" Beth Mikra 24, (th'sh'l't [1979]).

Hartmann, D., *Das Buch Rut in der Midrasch-literatur*, Leipzig, 1901.
Heidel, A., *The Gilgamesh Epic and Old Testament Parallels*, ed. 2, University of Chicago Press, Chicago, 1954.
Heschel, Abraham Joshua, quoting from the Zohar III in *The Sabbath; It's Meaning For Modern Man*, The Noonday Press, 1951.
Hook, S. H., ed., *Myth and Ritual*, Clarendon Press, London, 1933.
Idel, Moshe, *Kabbalah; New Perspectives*, Yale University, 1988.
Jastrow, M. Jr., "Moab," in *Dictionary of the Bible*, extra volume.
Jeremias, A., *Das Alte Testament im Lichte des Alten Orients*, ed4., Leipzig, 1920.
Johnson, A. R., "The Primary Meaning of *Go'el*," in *Supplements to Vetus Testamentum*, Leiden, 1953.
Joüon, Paul, *Ruth – Commentaire Philologique et Exegetique*, Rome, 1924.
Jung, C. G., *The Collected Works of C. G. Jung* (CW), Bollingen Series XX, Pantheon Press, New York.
— 1934, The Relations between the Ego and the Unconscious, in *Two Essays on Analytical Psychology*, 1953, CW 7.
— 1940 "Psychology and Religion" in *Psychology and Religion*, 1958, CW 11.
— 1946, "The Psychology of the Transference," in *The Practice of Psychotherapy*, ed. 2, 1966, CW 16.
— 1947, "Wotan," in *Civilization in Transition*, CW 10.
— 1949, "The Psychology of the Child Archetype," in CW 9i.
— 1953, *Psychology and Alchemy*, CW 12.
— 1954, "On the Nature of the Psyche," in *The Structure and Dynamics of the Psyche*, CW 8.
— 1955, "Synchronicity: an Acausal Principle." in *The Structure and Dynamics of the Psyche*, CW 8.
— 1949, "The Psychology of the Child Archetype" in *The Archetypes and the Collective Unconscious*, CW 9i.
— 1949, and Kerenyi, *Essays on a Science of Mythology*, Bollingen Foundation, Pantheon Press, New York, 1949.
Kerényi, C., 1949, (with C. G. Jung), *Essays on a Science of Mythology*, Bollingen Foundation, Pantheon Press, New York, 1949.
— , 1951, *The Gods of the Greeks*, Thames and Hudson, London and New York, 1951.
Kluckhohn, C., "Recurrent Themes in Myths and Mythmaking," in *The Making of Myth*, ed. R. N. Ohmann, G. P. Putnam's Sons, New York, 1962.
Kluger, H. Y., "Ruth, a Contribution to the Study of the Feminine Principle in the Old Testament," in *Spring*, New York, 1957.

Kluger, Rivkah Schärf, 1950, "The Image of Marriage Between God and Israel as it Occurs in the Old Testament, especially in Ezekiel XVI," in *Spring,* New York, 1950.

— 1976. *Satan in the Old Testament,* Northwestern University Press, Evanston, 1976.

— 1978, "Old Testament Roots of Woman's Spiritual Problem," *Journal of Analytical Psychology,* vol. 23, No. 2, 1978,

— 1991, *The Archetypal Significance of Gilgamesh,* Daimon Verlag, Einsiedeln, 1991.

— "Old Testament Roots of Woman's Spiritual Problem" and "The Idea of the Chosen People," *Psyche in Scripture,* Inner City Books, 1995.

Koehler, L., "Die Adoptionsform von Rt. 4:16," in *ZAW,* 29, 1909.

— and Baumgartner. W., *Lexicon in Veteris Testamenti Libros,* Leiden, 1958.

LaCocque, André, *The Feminine Unconventional: Four Subversive Figures in Israel's Tradition,* 1990.

Lehrman, S. M., "Hosea" in *The Twelve Prophets,* SBB, The Soncino Press, Bournemouth, Hants, 1948.

Lévi-Strauss, Claude, "The Structural Study of Myth" *Structural Anthropology,* 1967.

May, H. G., "Ruth's Visit to the High Place at Bethlehem," in *JRAS,* 1939.

Midrash Rabbah, ed2, translated and ed. by H. Freedman and M. Simon, 10 vol., Soncino Press, London and Bournemouth, 1951.

Morgenstern, J., "The Book of the Covenant," in *HUCA.,* 7, 1930.

Müller, E., *History of Jewish Mysticism,* Phaidon Press Ltd., Oxford, 1946.

Neumann, Erich, *The Child*, Shambhala, Boston, 1990.

Niditch, Susan, "The Wronged Woman Righted: an Analysis of Genesis 38": *Harvard Theological Review* 72, 1979, pp, 143-49.

Noth, M., "Die israelitische Personennamen im Rahmen der gemeinsemitischen Namengebung," in BWANT ed., R. Kittel, Stuttgart, 1928.

Patai, R., *Sex and Family in the Bible and the Middle East,* Doubleday Co., New York, 1959.

Riehm, E. C., *Handwörterbuch des Biblischen Altertums,* 2 vols., ed. 2, Leipzig, 1894.

Robertson, Edw., "The Plot of the Book of Ruth," in *BJRL,* vol. 32, 1949-50.

Robinson, H. Wheeler "The Hebrew Conception of Corporate Personality," in *BZAW,* 1936, 66.

Rowley, H. H., "The Marriage of Ruth," and "The Interpretation of the Song of Songs," both in *The Servant of the Lord and Other Essays,* London, 1952.

Rudolph, W., "Das Buch Ruth," in E. Sellin, ed., *Kommentar zum Alten Testament,* Leipzig, 1939.

Ruth Rabbah, volume 8 of *Midrash Rabbah,* see above.

Sasson, Jack M., *Ruth. A New Translation with Philological Commentary and a Formalist Folklorist Interpretation.* ed. 2, Sheffield Academic Press, Sheffield, 1989.

Schauss, Hayyim, *The Jewish Festivals,* Union of American Hebrew Congregations, Cincinnati, 1938.

Scholem, Gershom, *Major Trends in Jewish Mysticism,* Revised ed., Schocken Books, New York, 1946.

— *On the Kabbalah and Its Symbolism,* Routledge & Kegan Paul Ltd., London, 1965.

— *Sabbatai Sevi: The Mystical Messiah,* Princeton University Press, 1973.

— *Kabbalah,* Keter Publishing House, Jerusalem, Ltd., 1974.

— *Origins of the Kabbalah,* JPS, Princeton Univ., 1987.

— "Shekhinah," *On The Mystical Shape of the Godhead,* Schocken Books, New York, 1991.

Scott, R. B. Y., "The Pillars Jachin and Boaz," in *JBL,* 1939, **58**, 143f.

Slotki, I. W., "Kings" in S. B. B., Soncino Press, London and Bournemouth, 1950.

Slotki, J. L., "Ruth," *The Five Megilloth,* ed. A. Cohen, The Soncino Press, London and Bournemouth, 1952.

Smith, W. Robertson, *The Religion of the Semites,* (ed. 2 London, 1894.) Meridian edition, New York, 1956.

Staples, W. E., "The Book of Ruth," *AJSL,* 53, 1937.

Steinsaltz, Adin, *The Thirteen Petalled Rose,* trans. Yehuda haNegbi, Basic Books, Inc., New York, 1980.

Tanakh, The Holy Scriptures, Jewish Publication Society, Philadelphia, New York, Jerusalelm, 1988.

The Mystical Study of Ruth; Midrash Ha Ne'elam of the Zohar to the Book of Ruth, ed. Englander and Basser, Scholars Press, 1993.

Tishby, Isaiah, *The Wisdom of the Zohar, An Anthology of Texts,* The Littman Library, Oxford University Press, 1989.

— *The Wisdom of the Zohar; An Anthology of Texts,* Oxford University Press, 1989 (3 vols.).

Urbach, Ephraim E., *The Sages; Their Concepts and Beliefs,* The Magnes Press, The Hebrew University, Jerusalem, 1979.

Winckler, H., "Rut," in *Altorientalische Forschungen,* Leipzig, 1901.

Wolfenson, L. B., "The Character, Contents, and Date of Ruth," in *AJSL*, 27, 1910, 1911.

Woolley, Sir Leonard, *Digging up the Past*, Pelican Books, Harmondsworth, 1952.

Yaair Zakovitch, "Bain tmunoth haGoren b'M'gillath Ruth l'maaseh b'noth Lot." Shnathon 3, 1978-79.

Zakovitch, Yair, *Ruth: Introduction and Commentary*, Am Oved Publishers, Tel Aviv, 1990 (Hebrew).

(The) Zohar, 5 volumes, translated by H. Sperling and M. Simon, The Soncino Press, London & Bournemouth, 1949.

Zohar Ruth in *Zohar Chadash*, the Smyrna edition, 1878.

Abbreviations

AJSL American Journal of Semitic Languages and Literatures
B.C.E. Before the Common Era (same as B.C.)
BJRL Bulletin of the John Rylands Library
BWANT Beiträge zur Wissenschaft vom alten u. neuen Testament
BZAW Beihefte zur Zeitschrift für die A. T. Wissenschaft
D.B. Dictionary of the Bible, ed., J. Hastings
C.E. Common Era (same as A.D.)
CW Collected Works (of Jung)
E Elohist, one of the earlier Biblical texts
HUCA Hebrew Union College Annual
J Yahwistic, the earliest Biblical texts
JBL Journal of Biblical Literature
JRAS Journal of the Royal Asiatic Society of Great Britain and Ireland
SBB Soncino Books of the Bible
ZAW Zeitschrift für die alttestamentliche Wissenschaft

Subject Index

Author Index

Rivkah Schärf-Kluger

THE GILGAMESH EPIC

A Psychological Study
of a Modern Ancient Hero

Edited by H. Yehezkel Kluger
Foreword by C.A. Meier

The long-awaited life-long opus of
Jung's brilliant disciple, Rivkah Kluger,
this book consists of a detailed psychological commentary on the ancient
Sumero-Babylonian epic myth of Gilgamesh. The great beauty and depth of
the Gilgamesh epic, one of the world's
oldest known myths, render it a unique
instrument for learning about the human soul. Rivkah Kluger ably
applies it to illustrate the significance of myths for an understanding
of the development of consciousness and of religion: we are shown
how an ancient myth is highly relevant to the state of our world
today. (240 pp, illustrated, ISBN 3-85630-523-8)

Siegmund Hurwitz

LILITH – THE FIRST EVE

A Psychological Approach to Dark Aspects of the Feminine
Foreword by Marie-Louise von Franz

Jungian analyst and scholar Siegmund Hurwitz, who received his
training from C.G. Jung, Toni Wolff and M.-L. von Franz, wrote
his all-encompassing work on Lilith over a period of some 30 years.
On the basis of original texts, he presents the archetypal background of the myth of Lilith and shows the influences it has today
on the roles of modern men and women. An historical treatise
illustrated with modern case material and extremely well-received in
the years since its original publication in German, it at last becomes
accessible to English language readers.

(262 pages, ISBN 3-85630-522-X)

Ann Ulanov   – *The Wizards' Gate*
                 – *The Female Ancestors of Christ*
Ann & Barry Ulanov– *Cinderella and her Sisters*
Erlo van Waveren   – *Pilgrimage to the Rebirth*
Harry Wilmer   – *How Dreams Help*

Jungian Congress Papers:

Jerusalem 1983 – *Symbolic and Clinical Approaches*
Berlin 1986 – *Archetype of Shadow in a Split World*
Paris 1989 – *Dynamics in Relationship*
Chicago 1992 – *The Transcendent Function*
Zürich 1995 – *Open Questions in Analytical Psychology*
Florence 1998 – *Destruction and Creation: Personal and Cultural Transformations* (in preparation)

Daimon Books are available from your bookstore
or from our distributors:

In the United States:		*In Great Britain:*
Continuum & Cassell	Chiron Publications	Airlift Book Company
22883 Quicksilver Drive	400 Linden Avenue	8 The Arena
Dulles, VA 20166	Wilmette, IL 60091	Enfield, Middlesex EN3 7NJ
Phone: 1-800-561 7704	Phone: 800-397 8109	Phone: (0181) 804 0400
Fax: 1-703-661 1501	Fax: 847-256 2202	Fax: (0181) 804 0044

Worldwide:
Daimon Verlag
Hauptstrasse 85
CH-8840 Einsiedeln
Switzerland

Email: daimon@csi.com
http://ourworld.compuserve.com/homepages/daimon/